darkmatter

darkmatter

POEMS OF SPACE

edited by **Maurice Riordan**
and **Jocelyn Bell Burnell**

 CALOUSTE GULBENKIAN FOUNDATION

Published by the
Calouste Gulbenkian Foundation
United Kingdom Branch
email: info@gulbenkian.org.uk
website: www.gulbenkian.org.uk

Introduction and this selection © 2008 Maurice Riordan
and Jocelyn Bell Burnell.
Poems commissioned for this anthology © 2008
Julia Copus, Greg Delanty, James Fenton, Leontia Flynn,
John Kinsella, Antjie Krog, Nick Laird, Bill Manhire,
Kathryn Maris, John McAuliffe, Jamie McKendrick,
Paul Muldoon, Robert Pinsky, Deryn Rees-Jones,
Neil Rollinson and Tom Sleigh.
For copyright of all other poems see Acknowledgements,
p. 231.
The right of Maurice Riordan and Jocelyn Bell Burnell to
be identified as authors of the Introduction and editors of
this work has been asserted in accordance with the
Copyright, Designs and Patents Act 1988.

ISBN 978 1 903080 10 8

British Library Cataloguing-in-Publication Data
A catalogue record for this book is available from
the British Library

Designed by Helen Swansbourne
Typeset by Helen Robertson
Printed by Expression Printers Ltd, IP23 8HH

Distributed by Central Books,
99 Wallis Road, London E9 5LN
tel: 0845 458 9911, fax: 0845 458 9912
email: orders@centralbooks.com
website: www.centralbooks.co.uk

Contents

Preface

Dark Matter is the third of what has turned out to be a trilogy of anthologies of poems with scientific associations. *Wild Reckoning: An anthology provoked by Rachel Carson's 'Silent Spring'*, edited by poets John Burnside and Maurice Riordan, was the result of a project in which poets were asked to address that most poetic of themes, Nature – but in the light of growing concerns about climate change. The poets were paired with various environmental scientists, the poems written, and placed within the context of 100 poems, old and new, prescient in their regard for Nature's fragility.

Wild Reckoning met with much acclaim – Sir David King, then the Government's Chief Scientific Adviser, even picked it as his Desert Island Discs choice. It was followed by *Signs and Humours: The poetry of medicine*, edited by poet Lavinia Greenlaw, which used the same formula – new commissions set amongst a selection of ageless other poems – and was also well received.

The decision to produce a third anthology came when I happened to hear Jocelyn Bell Burnell on the radio admit to the fact that she collected poems about Space in her spare time. An essay on 'Astronomy and Poetry' in *Contemporary Poetry and Contemporary Science* (OUP 2006) confirmed her impeccable taste and we approached her to work with Maurice Riordan on this anthology. *Dark Matter* was almost an inevitable title and the collection is perhaps the most surreal and beguiling of the three, addressing, as it does, things beyond human worry. As in the other two cases, space scientists, astronomers, astrophysicists, cosmologists (their areas of study bafflingly specific to the outsider) were approached to impart a little of their knowledge to the poets.

Somewhere during this process I caught sight of some rather irritable correspondence, kicked off by a physicist who expressed scepticism about the possibility of any artist learning anything at all from a skimming visit to a boffin in a research facility. Instead he recommended a long-term residency which sounded as if it required a post-doc in physics just to begin. I disagreed with him. Poets are entitled to be snappers-up of unconsidered trifles, but they are no fools and many are well-read in intelligent popular science books at the very least. Who could not be intrigued by the profound implications of space science, its big bangs and phase transitions, its black holes and collapsed stars? And this is to say nothing of the metaphors and mental pictures that physicists themselves invent and relish. We know our knowledge is flimsy, mathematically inept, imaginatively limited. But we would be dull and blinkered beings if we didn't try to understand a little of what the scientists are arguing about – the age of the universe, expansion or steady state, dark material that is beyond human perception. These seem to be pertinent to our very existence and we must struggle with our grasp of them just as we might expect scientists to respect the profound historical knowledge and rigour required in writing good poetry.

I must thank Jocelyn Bell Burnell for sharing her passion with us – for space and for poetry – and Maurice Riordan for sharing his – for poetry and for space. I am very grateful to the sixteen poets and their science partners who appear to have enjoyed their encounters (notes on which appear on pages 218–29). And admiration goes to the artist Vija Celmins for the deceptively simple image on the cover – deceptive because her comet is not another Hubble photograph but a pencil drawing, as obsessively realised as any mathematical equation. Art meets science. Space meets poetry. Be astounded.

SIÂN EDE

Arts Director, Calouste Gulbenkian Foundation

Introduction

I ofen looked up at the sky an' assed meself the question –
what is the stars, what is the stars?

'CAPTAIN' BOYLE, *JUNO AND THE PAYCOCK*

People have been looking up at the sky and asking 'Captain' Boyle's question since time immemorial. Creation myths from around the globe and the world's major religions have offered one kind of response. The Psalmist sang out in praise: 'The Heavens declare the glory of God'. In Cherokee legend two dogs – one of them Canis Major – guard the path through the Milky Way to the land of souls. In our own European tradition the sailor, nomad and herdsman have looked up for three thousand years, not just to establish time or location but to see tales of pursuit and revenge, hubris, punishment or reward. The night sky was a canvas that integrated the human and supernatural in a seasonal drama. Even in my own childhood, Orion and his hound chased the hare across the crystalline skies of March.

One type of observer, however, has looked for empirical answers to 'Captain' Boyle's question – and in the process given a lead to scientific investigation. Since the Babylonians, astronomers have probed and mapped the heavens, developing ever more accurate instruments, and evolving over the centuries the sophisticated mathematics to express the movement and subtle relationships of heavenly bodies. The mythologised sky has long co-existed with this more scientific approach, one that has both troubled and excited the imagination with its discoveries. Some of the exotic ideas around nowadays have an ancient pedigree: Heraclitus believed that the basic stuff of the universe was fire, to which, periodically, it returned, and that the stars were bowls of the fiery element. He envisaged what cosmologists now call a 'closed universe'.

In contrast, the Roman poet Lucretius imagined space as limitless and Euclidean. And this was the accepted view throughout the centuries until Einstein. Space was an extension of everyday dimensions. But those parallel lines went on forever without converging. So they asked one to think of the impossible, to imagine infinity. The mind's eye travelled outwards until it came to what William Golding called 'the bounded mystery'.

The threshold of what is sayable is also the territory of poems. Poets perhaps are drawn towards utterance simply by looking up. Many have gone on space journeys, imagining, as Anna Laetitia Barbauld did in the 1770s (page 138):

> The desarts of creation, wide and wild;
> Where embryo systems and unkindled suns
> Sleep in the womb of chaos…

A hundred years previously Milton had Satan fly through the vast Copernican spaces revealed by the first telescopes – and perhaps something of the outcast angel's existential loneliness is reflected in their emptiness. Satan comes to rest on the Sun, which to the seventeenth-century imagination was a benignly radiant surface. John Hartley Williams, in the age of actual space travel, gives us a wonderfully comic variation of the fantastic journey with his 'Dan Dare at the Cosmos Ballroom' (page 145).

The exemplar of all such virtual journeys is, of course, the *Paradiso*, in which Dante ascends with Beatrice through the seven spheres. One of its celebrated episodes occurs when, at the end of Canto XXII, he looks back from the sphere of Saturn at the tiny earth 'that makes us all so fierce' (a moment elegantly recollected in Jamie McKendrick's 'Out There', page 163). Dante's cosmology is transcendent: the heavens are Heaven. But it also accords accurately with late-medieval astronomy and has some interesting features. His ascent brings him to the *primum mobile*, the boundary of the material world. It is a sort of 'event horizon' beyond which is the Empyrean, the unknowable realm of God. The *primum mobile* is the frontier of space and time, and moves inconceivably at infinite speed.

Modern science has transformed cosmology with a materialist concept of spacetime that likewise defeats our common sense. It seems we may exist, as Auden phrases it, 'a-straddle / An ever expanding saddle' (page 55). The Hubble universe – if it is a single entity and not part of an inaccessible multiverse – requires a geometry that we cannot visualise. Even observable space is a theatre of hard-to-imagine phenomena: vast balloons of supernovae exploding in slow motion, golf balls of incomprehensible density, our galaxy swirling about its own hungry black hole, while the other galaxies red-shift away at an accelerating gallop to god knows where – the whole shebang, it seems, glued together by some elusive stuff we call dark matter.

Luckily, we are sheltered from all this excitement. We live in a leafy suburb, an orderly place of mostly predictable events, where the sun 'rises' daily, the moon stays put in its orbit, and the constellations come and go in their seasons. It won't last, we know – the end will come to our dormitory backwater – but it will happen on a time-scale that makes the outcome un-urgent. In Robert Frost's words (page 25):

> … it wouldn't reward the watcher to stay awake
> In hopes of seeing the calm of heaven break
> On his particular time and personal sight.

Meanwhile, the system we know as life can continue to work against the grain of cosmic entropy. Radio telescopes still hearken to the heavens, astronomers map the distances to specific stars; new planets are spotted and comets predicted. There's time surely to figure out the secret of dark matter; still time to wonder and observe, for the human adventure to persist and, who knows, perhaps find some destiny that is as yet remote from our understanding.

One cannot think for long about such possibilities, and on such a scale, without the imagination being excited and stretched. The contemporary poet is no different from the Psalmist faced with the mystery of the sky. So an important aspect of the anthology was to ask poets to 'converse' with modern astronomers, astrophysicists and cosmologists. We wanted them to experience that primary sense of wonder in the context of the language and concepts of today's astronomy. More mundanely, we aimed for a good geographical spread of poets, with some from the southern hemisphere and North America, as well as those from the British Isles. Our hope was that the long tradition of poems concerned with the stars would be renewed and extended. We were pleasantly surprised by the intensity of engagement by both the poets and the scientists, and thrilled – as we expect readers will be – by the imaginative quality of the poems that emerged.

We have set this new work among a broad selection of poems that have drawn inspiration from the night sky. The sheer quantity and variety of poetry in the English canon devoted to astronomy meant we were spoilt for choice. We have given most room to poets – such as Milton, James Thomson and, in our time, Robert Frost – who have wrestled with the import of astronomical discoveries. But we have given space, too, to those poets who have exclaimed, or grieved, or just relieved themselves by moonlight; and to those who in love, like Shakespeare's Jessica and Lorenzo, have been moved to sit in admiration of 'the floor of heaven… inlaid with patens of bright gold' (page 175).

MAURICE RIORDAN

* * *

Dark matter, to the astronomer, is the invisible, massive, gravitating material that holds galaxies and clusters of galaxies together, whose nature we don't yet understand. We know there is more dark matter than radiant, and we understand enough to know that when its nature is recognised it will bring about a complete revolution in our conception of physics. Frederick Seidel and Rebecca Elson write about it, both with disquiet. Seidel's opening (page 191):

> It is the invisible
> Dark matter we are not made of
> That I am afraid of

sets the ominous tone for the rest of his poem. It is the unknown and unknowable that disturbs, and he has a good grip on the extent of our ignorance:

Dark matter is another
Matter. Cosmologists don't know.
The physicists do not.

Rebecca Elson, one of the very few professional astronomers to write poetry, knows that only dark matter can prevent our universe from flying apart, so she's anxiously searching for it (page 172):

For the dimmest stars,
For signs of unseen things:

To weigh us down.

The words 'dark matter', more widely used in a non-specialist way, also carry a sense that there are hidden depths to be plumbed and that exploration of them could be worthwhile.

For a number of years I worked 'up at Space' – the locals' name for the Mullard Space Science Laboratory near Dorking. It was an exciting period, as satellites were built and launched, to study the cosmos for the first time at wavelengths that the Earth's atmosphere screened out. Space Science refers mainly to the exploration of near-Earth space (what we used to call Outer Space, until our horizons shifted). Although satellites are now being sent further – to the outer edge of the Solar System – that's still a microscopically small distance compared to the size of the Universe.

Space has many meanings for me, but like other astronomers, I rarely use it to refer to the cosmos we study. As the daughter of an architect, space suggests for me the area defined by a building, or between buildings, or the layout of a town. As one of the generation of women who helped to change women's roles in Britain I know about giving someone space (i.e. freedom) to achieve. Then there's the emptiness, the space at the table, which also has connotations of opportunity. Pascal was much concerned by the emptiness of space (the Universe) – 'The eternal silence of these infinite spaces frightens me' – and William Empson uses this as a point of departure for his poem 'Letter I' (page 167). Others, including Leo Aylen, would concur with Pascal (page 151):

> Deep space blacks us
> Out from thought, drags us over the rim
>
> Of the known universe, into
> The beyond's private unconsciousness.

Although I don't use the word space to describe the Universe, it has for me suggestions of expanse and emptiness, and a blankness that gives scope for something.

And then there's inner space, as hard to understand as outer space, and more intimate (page 164):

> They cannot scare me with their empty spaces
> Between stars – on stars where no human race is.
> I have it in me so much nearer home
> To scare myself with my own desert places.   (*Robert Frost*)

It may be a desert place or it can be silent and deep, with unexpected, strong, currents. As a Quaker, used to silent worship, the cultivation of one's inner space (what Gwyneth Lewis calls 'our voyage along ourselves', page 115) is important to me, and poetry helps here. T. S. Eliot's 'Choruses from "The Rock"' (page 215) is a favourite:

> Endless invention, endless experiment,
> Brings knowledge of motion, but not of stillness;
> Knowledge of speech, but not of silence…

The exploration of inner space, the articulation of emotions, the development of intuition and self-knowledge can be difficult. Just as the universe needs dark matter, we need 'weight' to ground us, to hold together our experiences as we explore.

*

Research in astronomy in a leading university is exciting but demanding. The subject is fast-moving, dynamic and unpredictable, with new results rolling in each year and theories being overturned or rewritten. Our working culture requires total attention – it helps to be obsessive – and we don't talk much about interests outside the lab.

However, sometimes when academics in astronomy and physics reach a certain age their obsession with research abates a little, and other interests surface. These might concern the history or philosophy of science, or science and society or religion, or public outreach or (god forbid!) teaching undergraduates. Whatever it is, the young Turks in the department decide their senior colleague has gone off his or her rocker, and shake their heads sadly: he or she is now deemed fit only for teaching, administration or committee work. Knowing this, when I started 'collecting' poetry with an astronomical theme some twenty years ago, I kept very quiet about my hobby. It is only in the last few years that I have dared to 'come out'.

My role in the commissioning of poems for this anthology was to identify astronomers who might be willing to work one-to-one with a poet, serving as a scientific resource. As the first of my colleagues were approached, with what was for astronomers a most irregular request, I was unable to guess whether the idea would be met with derision or delight. Would they be interested? Would they be concerned about reputational risk? It was with great relief that I received those first prompt, positive responses and it has been heartening that so many colleagues have been so willing to take part in this unusual exercise, as well as delightful to see the results of the collaborations.

I am grateful to the Calouste Gulbenkian Foundation, and to Maurice Riordan, my co-editor, for this unique opportunity. Work which indulges one's hobby is always pleasurable and rewarding.

JOCELYN BELL BURNELL

The Commissioned Poems

Sixteen of these poems were commissioned by the Calouste Gulbenkian Foundation and were the result of discussions between poets and scientists. The following is a list of the poets and their scientific collaborators to whom we are grateful for their generosity with their time, expertise and advice.

JULIA COPUS: Malcolm Coe, Professor of Astronomy, School of Physics and Astronomy, University of Southampton

GREG DELANTY: David Helfand, Professor of Astronomy, Columbia University

JAMES FENTON: Pedro Ferreira, Lecturer in Astrophysics, University of Oxford

LEONTIA FLYNN: Mark Bailey MBE, Director, Armagh Observatory, Northern Ireland

JOHN KINSELLA: David Malin, Adjunct Professor of Scientific Photography, RMIT University, Melbourne

ANTJIE KROG: Hans Zinnecker, Head of the Star-Formation Group, Astrophysical Institute of Potsdam

NICK LAIRD: Paul Murdin, Senior Fellow, Institute of Astronomy, Cambridge

BILL MANHIRE: Marilyn Head, science writer

KATHRYN MARIS: Frank Close, Professor of Theoretical Physics, University of Oxford

JOHN McAULIFFE: John Dyson, Professor of Astronomy, University of Leeds

JAMIE McKENDRICK: Kevin Fong, Specialist Registrar in Anaesthesia and Intensive Care Medicine, University College London Hospitals, and Co-Director of the Centre for Altitude, Space and Extreme Environment (CASE) Medicine

PAUL MULDOON: Jo Dunkley, RCUK Research Fellow, University of Oxford

ROBERT PINSKY: Jim Moran, Donald H. Menzel Professor of Astrophysics, Harvard University, and Senior Radio Astronomer, Smithsonian Astrophysical Observatory

DERYN REES-JONES: Ian Morison, Gresham Professor of Astronomy, Jodrell Bank Centre for Astrophysics, University of Manchester

NEIL ROLLINSON: Anita Richards, AstroGrid Astronomer, Jodrell Bank Centre for Astrophysics, University of Manchester

TOM SLEIGH: Janna Levin, Professor of Physics and Astronomy, Barnard College, Columbia University

Particular thanks are also due to Siân Ede, Felicity Luard and Louisa Hooper for their help with every aspect of the book, to Helen Robertson and Helen Swansbourne for typesetting and design, and to Vija Celmins and The McKee Gallery for permission to use the cover image.

darkmatter

GERARD MANLEY HOPKINS

The Starlight Night

Look at the stars! look, look up at the skies!
  O look at all the fire-folk sitting in the air!
  The bright boroughs, the circle-citadels there!
Down in dim woods the diamond delves! the elves'-eyes!
The grey lawns cold where gold, where quickgold lies!
  Wind-beat whitebeam! air abeles set on a flare!
  Flake-doves sent floating forth at a farmyard scare! –
Ah well! it is all a purchase, all is a prize.

Buy then! bid then! – What? – Prayer, patience, alms, vows.
Look, look: a May-mess, like on orchard boughs!
  Look! March-bloom, like on mealed-with-yellow sallows!
These are indeed the barn; withindoors house
The shocks. This piece-bright paling shuts the spouse
  Christ home, Christ and his mother and all his hallows.

ANNE SEXTON

Riding the Elevator into the Sky

As the fireman said:
Don't book a room over the fifth floor
in any hotel in New York.
They have ladders that will reach further
but no one will climb them.
As the New York *Times* said:
The elevator always seeks out
the floor of the fire
and automatically opens
and won't shut.
These are the warnings
that you must forget
if you're climbing out of yourself.
If you're going to smash into the sky.

Many times I've gone past
the fifth floor,
cranking upward,
but only once
have I gone all the way up.
Sixtieth floor:
small plants and swans bending
into their grave.
Floor two hundred:
mountains with the patience of a cat,
silence wearing its sneakers.
Floor five hundred:
messages and letters centuries old,
birds to drink,
a kitchen of clouds.

Floor six thousand:
the stars,
skeletons on fire,
their arms singing.
And a key,
a very large key,
that opens something –
some useful door –
somewhere –
up there.

ROBERT FROST

On Looking up by Chance at the Constellations

You'll wait a long, long time for anything much
To happen in heaven beyond the floats of cloud
And the Northern Lights that run like tingling nerves.
The sun and moon get crossed, but they never touch,
Nor strike out fire from each other, nor crash out loud.
The planets seem to interfere in their curves,
But nothing ever happens, no harm is done.
We may as well go patiently on with our life,
And look elsewhere than to stars and moon and sun
For the shocks and changes we need to keep us sane.
It is true the longest drouth will end in rain,
The longest peace in China will end in strife.
Still it wouldn't reward the watcher to stay awake
In hopes of seeing the calm of heaven break
On his particular time and personal sight.
That calm seems certainly safe to last tonight.

WALT WHITMAN

On the Beach at Night

On the beach at night,
Stands a child with her father,
Watching the east, the autumn sky.

Up through the darkness,
While ravening clouds, the burial clouds, in black masses spreading,
Lower sullen and fast athwart and down the sky,
Amid a transparent clear belt of ether yet left in the east,
Ascends large and calm the lord-star Jupiter,
And nigh at hand, only a very little above,
Swim the delicate sisters the Pleiades.

From the beach the child holding the hand of her father,
Those burial-clouds that lower victorious soon to devour all,
Watching, silently weeps.

Weep not, child,
Weep not, my darling,
With these kisses let me remove your tears,
The ravening clouds shall not long be victorious,
They shall not long possess the sky, they devour the stars
    only in apparition,
Jupiter shall emerge, be patient, watch again another night,
    the Pleiades shall emerge,
They are immortal, all those stars both silvery and golden
    shall shine out again,
The great stars and the little ones shall shine out again, they endure,
The vast immortal suns and the long-enduring pensive moons
    shall shine again shine.

Then dearest child mournest thou only for Jupiter?
Considerest thou alone the burial of the stars?

Something there is,
(With my lips soothing thee, adding I whisper,
I give thee the first suggestion, the problem and indirection,)
Something there is more immortal even than the stars,
(Many the burials, many the days and nights, passing away,)
Something that shall endure longer even than lustrous Jupiter,
Or the radiant sisters the Pleiades.

JOSEPH ADDISON

Ode

The Spacious Firmament on high,
With all the blue Etherial Sky,
And spangled Heav'ns, a Shining Frame,
Their great Original proclaim:
Th' unwearied Sun, from Day to Day,
Does his Creator's Power display,
And publishes to every Land
The Works of an Almighty Hand.

Soon as the Evening Shades prevail,
The Moon takes up the wondrous Tale,
And nightly to the listning Earth
Repeats the Story of her Birth:
Whilst all the Stars that round her burn,
And all the Planets, in their turn,
Confirm the Tidings as they rowl,
And spread the Truth from Pole to Pole.

What though, in solemn Silence, all
Move round the dark terrestrial Ball?
What tho' nor real Voice nor Sound
Amid their radiant Orbs be found?
In Reason's Ear they all rejoice,
And utter forth a glorious Voice,
For ever singing, as they shine,
'The Hand that made us is Divine.'

WILLIAM HABINGTON

Nox Nocti Indicat Scientiam

When I survay the bright
    Cœlestiall spheare:
So rich with jewels hung, that night
Doth like an Æthiop bride appeare.

My soule her wings doth spread
    And heaven-ward flies,
Th'Almighty's Mysteries to read
In the large volumes of the skies.

For the bright firmament
    Shootes forth no flame
So silent, but is eloquent
In speaking the Creators name.

No unregarded star
    Contracts its light
Into so small a Charactar,
Remov'd far from our humane sight:

But if we stedfast looke,
    We shall discerne
In it as in some holy booke,
How man may heavenly knowledge learne.

It tells the Conqueror,
    That farre-stretcht powre
Which his proud dangers traffique for,
Is but the triumph of an houre.

That from the farthest North,
    Some Nation may
Yet undiscovered issue forth,
And ore his new got conquest sway.

    Some Nation yet shut in
      With hils of ice
May be let out to scourge his sinne
'Till they shall equall him in vice.

    And then they likewise shall
      Their ruine have,
For as your selves your Empires fall,
And every Kingdome hath a grave.

    Thus those Cœlestiall fires,
      Though seeming mute
The fallacie of our desires
And all the pride of life confute.

    For they have watcht since first
      The World had birth:
And found sinne in it selfe accurst,
And nothing permanent on earth.

JOHN McAULIFFE

Arguing about Stars near Inch

In a four-posted house, I glimpse
what looks like an axle-tree
hung with candles and lamps,
and draw, by firelight, a new geography.

On the hub of a burning wheel, you read
a twinkling, sidereal calendar.
Each keyhole of light has decreed
that we do not err or wander

even if I would square the telescope
and its multiplying suns
with the angel's flaming sword and the hope
that there's more to the world than common sense.

You say, as we walk the raised beach at Inch,
the world is nine tenths star.
But how do they begin, or finish?
What will it mean to see that far?

Which of us revels in the explosion of hydrogen,
the vault-crushing fact of origin?
The mediating rowan will drown;
dust and wind may well spoon,

shred or interlock each stellar ring, disc and jet,
each pulsar, dwarf,
straggler, gas giant and knot.
The names exceed us, the photograph

still develops. Twilight turns civil
then nautical, the sea silver and bright
to orange on purple.
The distant campuses go so starry with electric light

we hardly see the bodies of the sky move,
in time with us, through space,
unimaginably above
the dark room of this four-posted house.

BERNARD O'DONOGHUE

Timmy Buckley
Observes the Pleiades

It's January on a moonless, frosty night;
But they're not visible here, the ice-cluster
Sisters. They're hiding in North Cork
In '53, observed by Timmy Buckley
Who's waiting for the end of night milking
To fill his paper-stoppered whiskey bottle.

'The Seven Sisters, called the Pleiades,
Were the daughters of a famous king of Greece
Whose lands overflowed with milk and honey.
Electra was the fairest one of them.
There was this rich man in Kerry long ago
Who had a prize bull called Currens Atlas...'

Timmy had a name as a bit of a poet,
So we'd leave him to it. And once that's said,
Suddenly I see them here, low in the Bull
And realise they stood there all the time,
Waiting. I fix on them, knowing you're out as well
Watching, on whatever eminence.

Do you think that the eye's determined drawstring
That leads from me to them homes back to you,
As reliably as the mind's to Timmy Buckley? –
That such weightless communication
Influences the far receiving heart
To shrink the gap in space as well as time?

JULIA COPUS

Stars Moving Westwards in a Winter Garden

Perhaps the hardest thing about losing a lover is
to watch the year repeat its days

ANNE CARSON

Your birthday comes, then hers, leaves fall,
and drift against the freezing feet
of benches at the roadside, melt,

in all the colours of burnt wood,
into the edges of verges, lanes,
retreating underground, then re-

appear, supple as tongues,
awag among the branches, and the trees
are cock-a-hoop again. You can't

keep up; you're sick with it;
the Earth lies at a tilt,
and as it orbits tips its infinite

faces to the sun. By which
skewed means the seasons come,
the seasons go. You change

your hair, your wardrobe, friends, and take
to driving home the scenic route, the window
down. You take up smoking for a second time.

One night, a holy dark
December night of frost,
you stand in the garden, sleeplessness

hovering inside you like a planet.
Somewhere in your dark-adapted mind
you hear her calling to you

quietly, as if from an upstairs window.
You push your hands down, hard into their pockets,
lift your face to the heavens' stutters and glints.

Above you, the yellow lustre of Capella;
to your left, the twins, their close, in-leaning heads,
the giant, unseen shoulder of Orion.

You have heard it said
that when we look out into space
we're looking back in time.

Whose time? Our own?
For a moment you badly want this to mean
that the past itself is a kind of canopy

spread out on every side, in bluish black,
that somewhere in the night sky is contained,
among the million happenings

that led you here, that sudden summer storm
you sheltered from together, her small hand
too warm, too quick in yours (and yet

not nearly quick enough) beneath the oak
beside your uncle's house. How unforeseeable
those early intimacies were! And again how soon

unalterable. Or so they seemed.
So seems your present grief,
but grief also will pass – ripen and wither,

tied, as it is, like a moon, to this steady
turning of the earth through space,
away from the sun and back again, laden

with mountains, oceans, vineyards, quaysides, gardens,
and, for tonight, this one particular garden
where a man stands, breathing into the shape of his loss,

though in truth he could stand for any one of us:
earthbound, heart-sore, his boots in the frost-stiffened grass,
travelling eastwards, against a background of stars.

The Occultation of Orion

I saw, as in a dream sublime,
The balance in the hand of Time.
O'er East and West its beam impended;
And day, with all its hours of light,
Was slowly sinking out of sight,
While opposite, the scale of night
Silently with the stars ascended.

Like the astrologers of eld
In that bright vision I beheld
Greater and deeper mysteries.
I saw, with its celestial keys,
Its chords of air, its frets of fire
The Samian's great Æolian lyre
Rising through all its sevenfold bars
From earth unto the fixed stars.
And through the dewy atmosphere,
Not only could I see, but hear,
Its wondrous and harmonious strings,
In sweet vibration, sphere by sphere
From Dian's circle light and near,
Onward to vaster and wider rings,
Where, chanting through his beard of snows,
Majestic, mournful, Saturn goes,
And down the sunless realms of space
Reverberates the thunder of his bass.

Beneath the sky's triumphal arch
This music sounded like a march,
And with its chorus seemed to be

Preluding some great tragedy.
Sirius was rising in the east;
And, slow ascending one by one,
The kindling constellations shone.
Begirt with many a blazing star,
Stood the great giant Algebar,
Orion, hunter of the beast!
His sword hung gleaming by his side,
And, on his arm, the lion's hide
Scattered across the midnight air
The golden radiance of its hair.

The moon was pallid, but not faint;
And beautiful as some fair saint,
Serenely moving on her way
In hours of trial and dismay.
As if she heard the voice of God,
Unharmed with naked feet she trod
Upon the hot and burning stars,
As on the glowing coals and bars,
That were to prove her strength, and try
Her holiness and her purity.

Thus moving on, with silent pace,
And triumph in her sweet, pale face,
She reached the station of Orion.
Aghast he stood in strange alarm!
And suddenly from his outstretched arm
Down fell the red skin of the lion
Into the river at his feet,
His mighty club no longer beat
The forehead of the bull; but he
Reeled as of yore beside the sea,
When, blinded by Œnopion,
He sought the blacksmith at his forge

And, climbing up the mountain gorge,
Fixed his blank eyes upon the sun.

Then, through the silence overhead,
An angel with a trumpet said,
'Forevermore, forevermore,
The reign of violence is o'er!'
And, like an instrument that flings
Its music on another's strings,
The trumpet of the angel cast
Upon the heavenly lyre its blast,
And on from sphere to sphere the words
Re-echoed down the burning chords, –
'Forevermore, forevermore,
The reign of violence is o'er!'

ADRIENNE RICH

Orion

Far back when I went zig-zagging
through tamarack pastures
you were my genius, you
my cast-iron Viking, my helmed
lion-heart king in prison.
Years later now you're young

my fierce half-brother, staring
down from that simplified west
your breast open, your belt dragged down
by an oldfashioned thing, a sword
the last bravado you won't give over
though it weighs you down as you stride

and the stars in it are dim
and maybe have stopped burning.
But you burn, and I know it;
as I throw back my head to take you in
an old transfusion happens again:
divine astronomy is nothing to it.

Indoors I bruise and blunder,
break faith, leave ill enough
alone, a dead child born in the dark.
Night cracks up over the chimney,
pieces of time, frozen geodes
come showering down in the grate.

A man reaches behind my eyes
and finds them empty

a woman's head turns away
from my head in the mirror
children are dying my death
and eating crumbs of my life.

Pity is not your forte.
Calmly you ache up there
pinned aloft in your crow's nest,
my speechless pirate!
You take it all for granted
and when I look you back

it's with a starlike eye
shooting its cold and egotistical spear
where it can do least damage.
Breathe deep! No hurt, no pardon
out here in the cold with you
you with your back to the wall.

HART CRANE

Southern Cross

I wanted you, nameless Woman of the South,
No wraith, but utterly – as still more alone
The Southern Cross takes night
And lifts her girdles from her, one by one –
High, cool,
            wide from the slowly smoldering fire
Of lower heavens, –
               vaporous scars!

Eve! Magdalene!
          or Mary, you?

Whatever call – falls vainly on the wave.
O simian Venus, homeless Eve,
Unwedded, stumbling gardenless to grieve
Windswept guitars on lonely decks forever;
Finally to answer all within one grave!

And this long wake of phosphor,
               iridescent
Furrow of all our travel – trailed derision!
Eyes crumble at its kiss. Its long-drawn spell
Incites a yell. Slid on that backward vision
The mind is churned to spittle, whispering hell.

I wanted you… The embers of the Cross
Climbed by aslant and huddling aromatically.
It is blood to remember; it is fire
To stammer back… It is
God – your namelessness. And the wash –

All night the water combed you with black
Insolence. You crept out simmering, accomplished.
Water rattled that stinging coil, your
Rehearsed hair – docile, alas, from many arms.
Yes, Eve – wraith of my unloved seed!

The Cross, a phantom, buckled – dropped below the dawn.
Light drowned the lithic trillions of your spawn.

BILL MANHIRE

Herschel at the Cape

He steals the Dutch stars.
He will write with a pen.
He will write with light.

* *

1833: two months at sea.

Ashore, he notes
the mackerel drift of cloud.
His telescope stands in an orchard.

* *

Double star and double star.
He fixes the next nebula.

He rummages and sweeps.

Double star and double star.
He polishes the mirror.

* *

He cooks an egg in the sun
then moves on to mutton.

He studies tides, yet thinks time flies.
He loses the morning looking for a key.
He measures Alpha Centauri.

* *

Now he robs the wilds of lovely flowers.
He draws an outline and his wife paints in.

He shoots a few brown birds –
yellow beneath their tails –

then watches his children gather cones,
sketching until the Cape light fails.

Often he completes the background
but leaves the foreground empty…

Double star and double star –
a blank space, then a cluster.

  * *

He studies sun-spots.
The milk-boy steals the Beef.

He imitates the calls of birds.
He mistakes a cluster for a comet.

He makes another sweep.

  * *

And snakes attack, and dogs,
and *purgatorial* rats, and fleas.
There are coughs and colds
and a face-ache called the Sinkings.

And glorious nights, pure and clear
double star and double star
and sometimes such ill-adapted air
that the stars swell out and waver.

  * *

Also he studies weather.
His study is unroofed by wind.
Double star and double star.
He dismisses a carpenter.
He repairs a barometer.

⁎　⁎

He will propose the contact lens
and study colour blindness.

He will talk of snap-shot and of negative.
He will translate the *Iliad*.

He will be Master of the Mint.
He will invent the blueprint.

But at present he arranges stars.

⁎　⁎

He also evaporates the juice of figs.
He is quick in motion and in speech.
He draws a sudden gale.
He writes with the Anglo-Saxon thorn.
He digs in the earth. He does reductions.
He loves his wife and children.
He makes a zone and sweeps the sky.
And people with wings are walking on the moon!
(A hoax.) He is pestered in several languages.
He is modest, he is shy.
Halley can sometimes make him sigh...
it steals his sweeps, and makes him slow...
He uses the *camera lucida*.
He translates Michelangelo.

⁎　⁎

Four years at the Cape...
we hear his happiness from afar.

Of Saturn's sixth, uncertain moon,
he writes to his aunt with an italic shout:

'So this is *at last* a thing made out.'

      * *

Double star and double star.
Winter and summer.

      * *

Double star and double star.
He polishes the mirror.

JAMES FENTON

Cosmology: A Prologue

We know where the cauldrons were buried
And the axes, the flesh-hooks and the spits.
We know the site of the obsidian mines and the source of the
    chocolate flint.
But who put these questions first we will never know.

Who noticed the Sun rise in winter between the Wolf's Teeth
And thought to mark the summer's trajectory?
Who measured the shadow?
Who sank the great pits for the calendar stones?
Who kept in mind an ancient calculation
And served his tribe for a memory?

We know that the stars were constant to the navigator's eye
But who first remarked the planets in their retrograde motions,
Who first saw the sky as a question – that we do not know –
Or who first conceived the Earth as a general proposition.

When the season favoured the ships and the horizons were friendly,
When wind and current carried men forth like a desire,
And the village rounded on the young: 'Be gone, or be a burden
    to us,'
They found the old tales to be true, of land succeeding to land
And life beyond the promontory, places of distant wealth.

But who first thought of the moon as a place
In the sense that an archipelago is a place?
Who saw this place pass overhead?
Who viewed the sky as an archipelago
And the constellations as a clock?

Who enrolled in the night as in a university
And abandoned the archipelago,
Vanishing into the breakers one summer evening
Dedicating his destiny to the spheres?

We have marked the first lands to be beggared by tillage
And the epoch when sheep first yielded wool,
We can question the composition of a tooth,
We can fix the age of a splinter.
We are renowned for our superb equations.

But the music is lost that served the oarsmen for a metre
And the songs are forgotten that praised the Moon and the Sun
For the fourteen divisions of summer
While the winter months went nameless and unsung.

They built their ships not from a drawn design
But by a series of learned procedures.
They sang their boats into being.
They sang what they knew of the skies
And they sang the names of every visible star.

But who first said where I walk is Earth
And where I drown is Earth as well –
My hearth as a man, my roof-tree, my harbour, my grave?
Who first saw the Moon as an Earth at a distance?

All the evidence was destined to be lost –
Every chanted word, every sketch in the sand,
All thoughts committed to leaf and skin –
And this largest thought, this first cosmologist
Must have grasped for an instant before shying away from it,
Pushing it away from him to wait
As these questions have waited for their tens of thousands of seasons,
Patient or indifferent to our expertise.

from Orchestra

Behold the World, how it is whirled round,
And for it is so whirl'd, is named so;
In whose large volume many rules are found
Of this new Art, which it doth fairely show;
For your quicke eyes in wandring too and fro
 From East to West, on no one thing can glaunce,
 But if you marke it well, it seemes to daunce.

First you see fixt in this huge mirrour blew,
Of trembling lights, a number numberlesse:
Fixt they are nam'd, but with a name untrue,
For they all moove and in a Daunce expresse
That great long yeare, that doth containe no lesse
 Then threescore hundreds of those yeares in all,
 Which the sunne makes with his course naturall.

What if to you these sparks disordered seeme
As if by chaunce they had beene scattered there?
The gods a solemne measure doe it deeme,
And see a just proportion every where,
And know the points whence first their movings were;
 To which first points when all returne againe,
 The axel-tree of Heav'n shall breake in twaine.

Under that spangled skye, five wandring flames
Besides the King of Day, and Queene of Night,
Are wheel'd around, all in their sundry frames,
And all in sundry measures doe delight,
Yet altogether keepe no measure right;
   For by it selfe each doth it selfe advance,
   And by it selfe each doth a galliard daunce.

Venus, the mother of that bastard Love
Which doth usurpe the World's great Marshal's name,
Just with the sunne her dainty feete doth move,
And unto him doth all the jestures frame;
Now after, now afore, the flattering Dame,
   With divers cunning passages doth erre,
   Still him respecting that respects not her.

For that brave Sunne the Father of the Day,
Doth love this Earth, the Mother of the Night;
And like a revellour in rich array,
Doth daunce his galliard in his lemman's sight,
Both back, and forth, and sidewaies, passing light;
   His princely grace doth so the gods amaze,
   That all stand still and at his beauty gaze.

But see the Earth, when he approcheth neere,
How she for joy doth spring and sweetly smile;
But see againe her sad and heavy cheere
When changing places he retires a while;
But those blake cloudes he shortly will exile,
   And make them all before his presence flye,
   As mists consum'd before his cheerefull eye.

Who doth not see the measures of the Moone,
Which thirteene times she daunceth every yeare?
And ends her pavine thirteene times as soone
As doth her brother, of whose golden haire
She borroweth part, and proudly doth it weare;
  Then doth she coyly turne her face aside,
  Then halfe her cheeke is scarse sometimes discride.

Next her, the pure, subtile, and clensing Fire
Is swiftly carried in a circle even;
Though Vulcan be pronounst by many a lyer,
The only halting god that dwels in heaven:
But that foule name may be more fitly given
  To your false Fire, that farre from heaven is fall:
  And doth consume, waste, spoile, disorder all.

WILLIAM SHAKESPEARE

from Troilus and Cressida

I, iii, 84–109

ULYSSES:
The heavens themselves, the planets, and this centre
Observe degree, priority, and place,
Insisture, course, proportion, season, form,
Office, and custom, in all line of order;
And therefore is the glorious planet Sol
In noble eminence enthroned and sphered
Amidst the other; whose med'cinable eye
Corrects the influence of evil planets,
And posts like the commandment of a king,
Sans check to good and bad. But when the planets
In evil mixture to disorder wander,
What plagues, and what portents, what mutiny,
What raging of the sea, shaking of earth,
Commotion in the winds, frights, changes, horrors,
Divert and crack, rend and deracinate
The unity and married calm of states
Quite from their fixure! O, when degree is shaked,
Which is the ladder of all high designs,
The enterprise is sick! How could communities,
Degrees in schools, and brotherhoods in cities,
Peaceful commerce from dividable shores,
The primogeniture and due of birth,
Prerogative of age, crowns, sceptres, laurels,
But by degree stand in authentic place?
Take but degree away, untune that string,
And hark what discord follows.

W.H. AUDEN

After Reading a Child's Guide to Modern Physics

If all a top physicist knows
About the Truth be true,
Then, for all the so-and-so's,
Futility and grime,
Our common world contains,
We have a better time
Than the Greater Nebulae do,
Or the atoms in our brains.

Marriage is rarely bliss
But, surely, it would be worse
As particles to pelt
At thousands of miles per sec
About a universe
In which a lover's kiss
Would either not be felt
Or break the loved one's neck.

Though the face at which I stare
While shaving it be cruel
For, year after year, it repels
An ageing suitor, it has,
Thank God, sufficient mass
To be altogether there,
Not an indeterminate gruel
Which is partly somewhere else.

Our eyes prefer to suppose
That a habitable place
Has a geocentric view,
That architects enclose
A quiet euclidean space:
Exploded myths – but who
Would feel at home a-straddle
An ever expanding saddle?

The passion of our kind
For the process of finding out
Is a fact one can hardly doubt,
But I would rejoice in it more
If I knew more clearly what
We wanted knowledge for,
Felt certain still that the mind
Is free to know or not.

It has chosen once, it seems,
And whether our concern
For magnitude's extremes
Really becomes a creature
Who comes in a median size,
Or politicising Nature
Be altogether wise,
Is something we shall learn.

LOUIS SIMPSON

Physical Universe

He woke at five and, unable
to go back to sleep,
went downstairs.

A book was lying on the table
where his son had done his homework.
He took it into the kitchen,
made coffee, poured himself a cup,
and settled down to read.

'There was a local eddy in the swirling gas
of the primordial galaxy,
and a cloud was formed, the protosun,
as wide as the present solar system.

This contracted. Some of the gas
formed a diffuse, spherical nebula,
a thin disk, that cooled and flattened.
Pulled one way by its own gravity,
the other way by the sun,
it broke, forming smaller clouds,
the protoplanets. Earth
was 2000 times as wide as it is now.'

The earth was without form, and void,
and darkness was upon the face of the deep.

* * *

'Then the sun began to shine,
dispelling the gases and vapors,

shrinking the planets, melting earth,
separating iron and silicate
to form the core and mantle.
Continents appeared…'
history, civilisation,
the discovery of America
and the settling of Green Harbor,
bringing us to Tuesday, the seventh of July.

Tuesday, the day they pick up the garbage!
He leaped into action,
took the garbage bag out of its container,
tied it with a twist of wire,
and carried it out to the tool-shed,
taking care not to let the screen-door slam,
and put it in the large garbage-can
that was three-quarters full.
He kept it in the tool-shed so the raccoons
couldn't get at it.

He carried the can out to the road,
then went back into the house
and walked around, picking up newspapers
and fliers for: 'Thompson Seedless Grapes,
California's finest sweet eating';

'Scott Bathroom Tissue';

'Legislative report from Senator Ken LaValle.'

He put all this paper in a box,
and emptied the waste baskets in the two
downstairs bathrooms,
and the basket in the study.

He carried the box out to the road,
taking care not to let the screen-door slam,
and placed the box next to the garbage.

Now let the garbage men come!

* * *

He went back upstairs.
Susan said, 'Did you put out the garbage?'
But her eyes were closed.
She was sleeping, yet could speak in her sleep,
ask a question, even answer one.

'Yes,' he said, and climbed into bed.
She turned around to face him,
with her eyes still closed.

He thought, perhaps she's an oracle,
speaking from the Collective Unconscious.
He said to her, 'Do you agree with Darwin
that people and monkeys have a common ancestor?
Or should we stick to the Bible?'

She said, 'Did you take out the garbage?'

'Yes,' he said, for the second time.
Then he thought about it. Her answer
had something in it of the sublime.
Like a *koan*... the kind of irrelevance
a Zen-master says to the disciple
who is asking riddles of the universe.

He put his arm around her,
and she continued to breathe evenly
from the depths of sleep.

T.E. HULME

Autumn

A touch of cold in the Autumn night –
I walked abroad,
And saw the ruddy moon lean over a hedge
Like a red-faced farmer.
I did not stop to speak, but nodded,
And round about were the wistful stars
With white faces like town children.

D.H. LAWRENCE

Southern Night

Come up, thou red thing.
Come up, and be called a moon.

The mosquitoes are biting to-night
Like memories.

Memories, northern memories,
Bitter-stinging white world that bore us
Subsiding into this night.

Call it moonrise
This red anathema?

Rise, thou red thing,
Unfold slowly upwards, blood-dark;
Burst the night's membrane of tranquil stars
Finally.

Maculate
The red Macula.

PERCY BYSSHE SHELLEY

from Letter to Maria Gisborne

                    I recall
My thoughts, and bid you look upon the night.
As water does a sponge, so the moonlight
Fills the void, hollow, universal air –
What see you? – unpavilioned Heaven is fair,
Whether the moon, into her chamber gone,
Leaves midnight to the golden stars, or wan
Climbs with diminished beams the azure steep;
Or whether clouds sail o'er the inverse deep,
Piloted by the many-wandering blast,
And the rare stars rush through them dim and fast: –
All this is beautiful in every land. –
But what see you besides? – a shabby stand
Of Hackney coaches – a brick house or wall
Fencing some lonely court, white with the scrawl
Of our unhappy politics; – or worse –
A wretched woman reeling by, whose curse
Mixed with the watchman's, partner of her trade,
You must accept in place of serenade –
Or yellow-haired Pollonia murmuring
To Henry, some unutterable thing.
I see a chaos of green leaves and fruit
Built round dark caverns, even to the root
Of the living stems that feed them – in whose bowers
There sleep in their dark dew the folded flowers;
Beyond, the surface of unsickled corn
Trembles not in the slumbering air, and borne
In circles quaint, and ever-changing dance,
Like wingèd stars the fire-flies flash and glance,
Pale in the open moonshine, but each one

Under the dark trees seems a little sun,
A meteor tamed; a fixed star gone astray
From the silver regions of the milky way; –
Afar the Contadino's song is heard,
Rude, but made sweet by distance – and a bird
Which cannot be the Nightingale, and yet
I know none else that sings so sweet as it
At this late hour; – and then all is still –
Now – Italy or London, which you will!

BEN JONSON

from Cynthia's Revels

Queen and huntress, chaste, and fair,
Now the sun is laid to sleep,
Seated, in thy silver chair,
State in wonted manner keep:
　　Hesperus entreats thy light,
　　Goddess, excellently bright.

Earth, let not thy envious shade
Dare itself to interpose;
Cynthia's shining orb was made
Heaven to clear, when day did close:
　　Bless us then with wishèd sight,
　　Goddess, excellently bright.

Lay thy bow of pearl apart,
And thy crystal-shining quiver;
Give unto the flying hart
Space to breathe, how short soever:
　　Thou, that mak'st a day of night,
　　Goddess, excellently bright.

SIR PHILIP SIDNEY

With how sad steps, ô Moone, thou climb'st the skies

With how sad steps, ô Moone, thou climb'st the skies,
   How silently, and with how wanne a face,
   What, may it be that even in heav'nly place
That busie archer his sharpe arrowes tries?
Sure, if that long with *Love* acquainted eyes
   Can judge of *Love*, thou feel'st a Lover's case;
   I reade it in thy lookes, thy languisht grace,
To me that feele the like, thy state descries.
   Then ev'n of fellowship, ô Moone, tell me
Is constant *Love* deem'd there but want of wit?
Are Beauties there as proud as here they be?
Do they above love to be lov'd, and yet
   Those Lovers scorne whom that *Love* doth possesse?
   Do they call *Vertue* there ungratefulnesse?

PHILIP LARKIN

Sad Steps

Groping back to bed after a piss
I part thick curtains, and am startled by
The rapid clouds, the moon's cleanliness.

Four o'clock: wedge-shadowed gardens lie
Under a cavernous, a wind-picked sky.
There's something laughable about this,

The way the moon dashes through clouds that blow
Loosely as cannon-smoke to stand apart
(Stone-coloured light sharpening the roofs below)

High and preposterous and separate –
Lozenge of love! Medallion of art!
O wolves of memory! Immensements! No,

One shivers slightly, looking up there.
The hardness and the brightness and the plain
Far-reaching singleness of that wide stare

Is a reminder of the strength and pain
Of being young; that it can't come again,
But is for others undiminished somewhere.

TED HUGHES

Full Moon and Little Frieda

A cool small evening shrunk to a dog bark and the clank of a bucket –

And you listening.
A spider's web, tense for the dew's touch.
A pail lifted, still and brimming – mirror
To tempt a first star to a tremor.

Cows are going home in the lane there, looping the hedges
    with their warm wreaths of breath –
A dark river of blood, many boulders,
Balancing unspilled milk.

'Moon!' you cry suddenly, 'Moon! Moon!'

The moon has stepped back like an artist gazing amazed at a work

That points at him amazed.

LEONTIA FLYNN

The Full Moon and the Ferris Wheel

They've put up a Ferris wheel, some sixty metres high
beside the old town hall – a wonder of construction,
its metal spokes gleaming. Behind it in the sky,
her size a trick, in league with the horizon,
is the bright disc of a massive harvest moon.

The wheel rotates. The moon also rotates
In tune, however, with the earth's rotation.
A force has slowed that billiard ball, the moon
– a torque, or fan-belt grinding down the seas –
and locked these spheres. Her far side keeps its distance.

The far side of the moon is not the dark side:
her open face and plains – the kicking mule
and landing sites – are all we'll ever know.
Thus ogled and probed, the moon remains endlessly public.
Her fate spectacular, as is the Ferris wheel's.

The Moon and the Yew Tree

This is the light of the mind, cold and planetary.
The trees of the mind are black. The light is blue.
The grasses unload their griefs on my feet as if I were God,
Prickling my ankles and murmuring of their humility.
Fumy, spiritous mists inhabit this place
Separated from my house by a row of headstones.
I simply cannot see where there is to get to.

The moon is no door. It is a face in its own right,
White as a knuckle and terribly upset.
It drags the sea after it like a dark crime; it is quiet
With the O-gape of complete despair. I live here.
Twice on Sunday, the bells startle the sky –
Eight great tongues affirming the Resurrection.
At the end, they soberly bong out their names.

The yew tree points up. It has a Gothic shape.
The eyes lift after it and find the moon.
The moon is my mother. She is not sweet like Mary.
Her blue garments unloose small bats and owls.
How I would like to believe in tenderness –
The face of the effigy, gentled by candles,
Bending, on me in particular, its mild eyes.

I have fallen a long way. Clouds are flowering
Blue and mystical over the face of the stars.
Inside the church, the saints will be all blue,
Floating on their delicate feet over the cold pews,
Their hands and faces stiff with holiness.
The moon sees nothing of this. She is bald and wild.
And the message of the yew tree is blackness – blackness and silence.

THOMAS HARDY

At a Lunar Eclipse

Thy shadow, Earth, from Pole to Central Sea,
Now steals along upon the Moon's meek shine
In even monochrome and curving line
Of imperturbable serenity.

How shall I link such sun-cast symmetry
With the torn troubled form I know as thine,
That profile, placid as a brow divine,
With continents of moil and misery?

And can immense Mortality but throw
So small a shade, and Heaven's high human scheme
Be hemmed within the coasts yon arc implies?

Is such the stellar gauge of earthly show,
Nation at war with nation, brains that teem,
Heroes, and women fairer than the skies?

ROBINSON JEFFERS

OCT. 27 Lunar Eclipse – 98%
(On the Calendar)

The moon went naked to-night, she thought she was hid
In the earth shadow,
Shy and so trustful
She drew off the shining veil, slowly, slowly,
From the dove breasts
To the white feet,
All her pearly body
(There was light enough)
Breathing and bare
Stood undefended,
One saw again how much more beautiful is beauty
When the jewels and shining
Clothes are laid down.

SAMUEL BUTLER

from The Elephant in the Moon

A learned society of late,
The glory of a foreign state,
Agreed, upon a summer's night,
To search the Moon by her own light;
To make an inventory of all
Her real estate, and personal;
And make an accurate survey
Of all her lands, and how they lay,
As true as that of Ireland, where
The sly surveyors stole a shire:
T'observe her country, how 'twas planted,
With what sh'abounded most, or wanted;
And make the proper'st observations
For settling of new plantations,
If the society should incline
T'attempt so glorious a design.
   This was the purpose of their meeting,
For which they chose a time as fitting;
When at the full her radiant light
And influence too were at their height.
And now the lofty tube, the scale
With which they heaven itself assail,
Was mounted full against the Moon;
And all stood ready to fall on,
Impatient who should have the honour
To plant an ensign first upon her.
When one, who for his deep belief
Was virtuoso then in chief,
Approved the most profound, and wise,
To solve impossibilities,

Advancing gravely, to apply
To th' optic glass his judging eye,
Cried, 'Strange!' – then reinforced his sight
Against the Moon with all his might,
And bent his penetrating brow,
As if he meant to gaze her through;
When all the rest began t'admire,
And, like a train, from him took fire,
Surprised with wonder, beforehand,
At what they did not understand,
Cried out, impatient to know what
The matter was they wondered at.

    Quoth he, 'Th' inhabitants o' th' Moon,
Who, when the Sun shines hot at noon,
Do live in cellars underground,
Of eight miles deep, and eighty round,
In which at once they fortify
Against the sun and th' enemy,
Which they count towns and cities there,
Because their people's civiller
Than those rude peasants, that are found
To live upon the upper ground,
Called Privolvans, with whom they are
Perpetually in open war;
And now both armies, highly enraged,
Are in a bloody fight engaged,
And many fall on both slides slain,
As by the glass 'tis clear, and plain.
Look quickly then, that every one
May see the fight before 'tis done,'
    With that a great philosopher,
Admired, and famous far and near,
As one of singular invention,
But universal comprehension,

Applied one eye, and half a nose
Unto the optic engine close.

Quoth he, 'A stranger sight appears
Than e'er was seen in all the spheres,
A wonder more unparalleled,
Than ever mortal tube beheld;
An elephant from one of those
Two mighty armies is broke loose,
And with the horror of the fight
Appears amazed, and in a fright;
Look quickly, lest the sight of us
Should cause the startled beast t' imboss.
It is a large one, far more great
Than e'er was bred in Afric yet;
From which we boldly may infer,
The Moon is much the fruitfuller.

'Most excellent and virtuous friends,
This great discovery makes amends
For all our unsuccessful pains,
And lost expense of time and brains.
For, by this sole phenomenon,
We 'ave gotten ground upon the Moon;
And gained a pass, to hold dispute
With all the planets that stand out;
To carry out this most virtuous war
Home to the door of every star,
And plant th' artillery of our tubes
Against their proudest magnitudes…'

This said, they all with one consent,
Agreed to draw up th' instrument,
And, for the general satisfaction,
To print it in the next 'Transaction'.

But, whilst the chiefs were drawing up
This strange memoir o' th' telescope,
One, peeping in the tube by chance,
Beheld the elephant advance.
And, from the west side of the Moon
To th' east was in a moment gone.
This being related, gave a stop
To what the rest were drawing up;
And every man, amazed anew
How it could possibly be true,
That any beast should run a race
So monstrous, in so short a space,
Resolved, howe'er, to make it good,
At least, as possible as he could;
And rather his own eyes condemn,
Than question what he 'ad seen with them…

But, while they were diverted all
With wording the memorial,
The footboys, for diversion too,
As having nothing else to do,
Seeing the telescope at leisure,
Turned virtuosos for their pleasure;
Began to gaze upon the Moon,
As those they waited on, had done,
With monkeys' ingenuity,
That love to practise what they see;
When one, whose turn it was to peep,
Saw something in the engine creep;
And, viewing well, discovered more
Than all the learned had done before.
Quoth he, 'A little thing is slunk
Into the long star-gazing trunk;
And now is gotten down so nigh,
I have him just against mine eye.'

This being overheard by one,
Who was not so far overgrown
In any virtuous speculation,
To judge with mere imagination,
Immediately he made a guess
At solving all appearances,
A way far more significant,
Than all their hints of th'elephant,
And found, upon a second view,
His own hypothesis most true;
For he had scarce applied his eye
To th'engine, but immediately
He found a mouse was gotten in
The hollow tube, and, shut between
The two glass windows in restraint
Was swelled into an elephant;
And proved the virtuous occasion
Of all this learnèd dissertation;
And, as a mountain heretofore
Was great with child, they say, and bore
A silly mouse; this mouse, as strange,
Brought forth a mountain in exchange.

W.H. AUDEN

Moon Landing

It's natural the Boys should whoop it up for
so huge a phallic triumph, an adventure
    it would not have occurred to women
    to think worth while, made possible only

because we like huddling in gangs and knowing
the exact time: yes, our sex may in fairness
    hurrah the deed, although the motives
    that primed it were somewhat less than *menschlich*.

A grand gesture. But what does it period?
What does it osse? We were always adroiter
    with objects than lives, and more facile
    at courage than kindness: from the moment

the first flint was flaked this landing was merely
a matter of time. But our selves, like Adam's,
    still don't fit us exactly, modern
    only in this – our lack of decorum.

Homer's heroes were certainly no braver
than our Trio, but more fortunate: Hector
    was excused the insult of having
    his valor covered by television.

Worth *going* to see? I can well believe it.
Worth *seeing*? Mneh! I once rode through a desert
    and was not charmed: give me a watered
    lively garden, remote from blatherers

about the New, the von Brauns and their ilk, where
on August mornings I can count the morning
    glories, where to die has a meaning,
    and no engine can shift my perspective.

Unsmudged, thank God, my Moon still queens the Heavens
as She ebbs and fulls, a Presence to glop at,
    Her Old Man, made of grit not protein,
    still visits my Austrian several

with His old detachment, and the old warnings
still have power to scare me: Hybris comes to
    an ugly finish, Irreverence
    is a greater oaf than Superstition.

Our apparatniks will continue making
the usual squalid mess called History:
    all we can pray for is that artists,
    chefs and saints may still appear to blithe it.

August 1969

Listening

I

As our metal eyes wake
to absolute night,
where whispers fly
from the beginning of time,
we cup our ears to the heavens.
We are listening

on the volcanic rim of Flagstaff
and in the fields beyond Boston,
in a great array that blooms
like coral from the desert floor,
on highwire webs patrolled
by computer spiders in Puerto Rico.

We are listening for a sound
beyond us, beyond sound,

searching for a lighthouse
in the breakwaters of our uncertainty,
an electronic murmur,
a bright, fragile *I am.*

Small as tree frogs
staking out one end
of an endless swamp,
we are listening
through the longest night
we imagine, which dawns
between the life and times of stars.

II

Our voice trembles
with its own electric,
we who mood like iguanas,
we who breathe sleep
for a third of our lives,
we who heat food
to the steaminess of fresh prey,
then feast with such
good manners it grows cold.

In mind gardens
and on real verandas
we are listening,
rapt among the Persian lilacs
and the crickets,
while radio telescopes
roll their heads, as if in anguish.

With our scurrying minds
and our lidless will
and our lank, floppy bodies
and our galloping yens
and our deep, cosmic loneliness
and our starboard hearts
where love careens,
we are listening,
the small bipeds
with the giant dreams.

DEREK MAHON

Mt Gabriel

As if planted there by giant golfers in the skies,
White in the gloaming, last before New Brunswick,
The geodesic domes have left their caves
To sit out in the summer sunset. Angels
Beamed at Namancos and Bayona, sick
With exile, they yearn homeward now, their eyes
Tuned to the ultramarine, first-star-pierced dark
Reflected on the dark, incoming waves –
Who, aliens, burnt-out meteorites, time capsules,
Are here for ever now as intermediaries
Between the big bang and our scattered souls.

ROBERT PINSKY

The Procession

At the summit of Mauna Kea, an array of antennae
Sensitive to the colors of invisible light.

The antennae sidle heavily on motors to measure
Submillimeter waves across the cold universe,

In patterns choreographed by an astronomer's hand
At a computer in Massachusetts, in real time:

A system of waves and removes and extremes
Devoted to the wavering, remote nature of things.

Also, your soul. Your father Adam known as Vishnu
And Lakshmi your mother known also as Eve,

Both of them smaller than the width of a hair,
Are riding astride matched tortoises along a road

Nine microns wide, following another Eve
And another Adam in a long procession

Of mothers and fathers, Lakshmis and Vishnus
With you their child Cain and their child Abel.

Innumerable their names and doings, innumerable
Their destinies and remote histories and tongues.

Somewhere among them your ancestor the slave
Also your ancestors the king the thief the stranger.

The immense agonies of my tiny span of life:
A pause as one tortoise in the chain lifts his foot

To tread the emanation of a dead star, still alive
And afire when the procession first set out.

Everyone alive the outcome of a rape,
Everyone alive the outcome of a great love.

Cain and Abel, Heloise and Abelard, mostly
Anonymous they travel a filament of light

To cross the Nothing between the galaxies
Into the pinhole iris of your mortal eye.

At the heart of each telescope on Mauna Kea,
An aperture finer than a hair on Vishnu's head.

On every hair on each Vishnu's head, a procession
Of tiny paired tortoises crossing a galactic distance.

In the skull of each tortoise in the long procession,
A faceted jewel attuned to a spectral channel

Where endlessly Kronos eats us his children, suffering
By nature each of us in a certain sliver of time.

MIROSLAV HOLUB

Night at the observatory

It was thawing.
As if the Avars
were attacking underground.

They stood leaning in the shadows,
his finger discovered
an inch
of unknown gentle country
beneath her left shoulder,

Atlantis, he said,
Atlantis.

> Above the fields the wires hissed like iguanas.
> A car's horn faded on the air
> like a voice from Greek tragedy.
> Behind the walls the guard paced back and forth.
> Hares were sniffing the distant town.
> Wood rotted in the ground.
> The Avars were winning.
> Trees cracked at the joints.
> The wind came and veered off.
> They kissed.

> From somewhere a rock was falling
> its second thousand years.
> And the stars were taking in
> signals on a frequency of ten megacycles,
> beamed to a civilisation
> which had died
> just before the dawn
> of eternity.

PATRIC DICKINSON

Jodrell Bank

Who were they, what lonely men
Imposed on the fact of night
The fiction of constellations
And made commensurable
The distances between
Themselves their loves and their doubt
Of governments and nations;
Who made the dark stable

When the light was not? Now
We receive the blind codes
Of spaces beyond the span
Of our myths, and a long dead star
May only echo how
There are no loves nor gods
Men can invent to explain
How lonely all men are.

JEAN SPRACKLAND

Lovell Radio Telescope, Jodrell Bank

Clouds scan it at a careful pace,
absorbing its data until they're saturated.
They roll over the fields
and let some of it fall raining onto the grass.
It runs into the earth
with a soft desolate sound.

There's a quiet here, like intelligence.
The cows have a look of wounded surprise
from eating the clever grass,
full of knowledge they don't know how to use.
The buttercups are a special shade of yellow,
unnaturally bright with information.
The trees are more attentive.
Insects make thoughtful moves like chess pieces.

Those clouds are pure whipped memory;
they read and count and store without understanding.
Behind them, a blue which is really darkness
reeling with a million clumsy signals.

NORMAN NICHOLSON

The Undiscovered Planet

Out on the furthest tether let it run
Its hundred-year-long orbit, cold
As solid mercury, old and dead
Before this world's fermenting bread
Had got a crust to cover it; landscape of lead
Whose purple voes and valleys are
Lit faintly by a sun
No nearer than a measurable star.

No man has seen it; nor the lensed eye
That pinpoints week by week the same patch of sky
Records even a blur across its pupil; only
The errantry of Saturn, the wry
Retarding of Uranus, speak
of the pull beyond the pattern:
The unknown is shown
Only by a bend in the known.

DIANA SYDER

The Naming of Neptune

for Mick and Sara

Why Neptune? In what way was it fluid, this speck
in the sky, and what alternatives were there? Strange

how Neptune suits it, that it does have oceanic qualities
and now nothing else would do, as if we crave

our gods, our magic, after all. But I've never
seen it and probably never will, so the only difference

is that now there's a neural pathway and Neptune
has an atmosphere in the deep space of my head.

ALISON HAWTHORNE DEMING

Mt Lemmon,
Steward Observatory, 1990

What it takes to dazzle us, masters of dazzle,
all of us here together at the top of the world,
is a night without neon or mercury lamps.
Black sheen flowing above,
the stars, unnamed and disorderly –
diamonds, a ruby or sapphire,
scattered and made
more precious for being cut
from whatever strand
once held them together.
The universe is emptiness and dust,
occasional collisions, collapsing zones of gas,
electrical bursts, and us.

Here is the 60-inch scope where
we struggle to see one pinpoint of light,
each singularity with its timid twinkle
become a city of stars, that trapezoidal
grouping at the end of Orion's sword,
a cloudy nursery spawning
galactic stuff, lit but not illuminated
by a glassy hot blue star. What is it to see?
A mechanism wired in the brain
that leads to wonder. What is it
to wonder but to say
what we've seen and, having said it,
need to see farther.

Here are the globulars and spirals,
the dumbbell, ring, and crab – particles
swept like water in a drain, shapes
mapping the torque that shapes them,
tension of matter, micro- and
macro-scopic, orbiting, electron
and planet straining at apogee
like a husky on the leash.
Here is Pegasus, the Great Square –
call it the Baseball Diamond, a story
we can see, one we can use
to find our way back. A scientist
can say *NGC 5194/5* to another
and the other says *Ahhh*,
picturing the massive whirlpool, its
small companion galaxy eddying by its side.

Call it the Nipple with a nearby Mole,
call it the Chief Executive Officer
walking his Spitz. Describing *is* imagining –
knowing, not knowing but
having the language
to convey, to *be* the water carrier,
Aquarius, to quench another.
I saw it with my own eyes.
Seeing is believing.
That paloverde tree is green.
On earth as it is in heaven.
But the sky is not blue
and the stars are not a drifting dome,
merely coordinates plotted on
the immensity inside –
the Eternity we walk in when we dream.

Still the universe (the way we see it)
is more real than Heraclitus,
who said the stars were solid bowls
filled with fire, fire which feeds
on the ocean's watery breath.
Why not, since water is consumed
by fire, imagine it as food?
Why not think the brain's
favorite food is seeing?
We still don't know what light is.
Where matter comes from. How the dust
became fire. Why our fire must
turn to dust. And all we have to go on
(refining the instrument) is our selves –
the skin at the tips of our fingers.

All we have to go on is ignorance –
to pay attention to what we've missed.
tides? Amorph –
one scientist's notation in
The Atlas of Galaxies
beneath a shapeless smudge.
They have to take it seriously, everything
they see, trying to invent
a way to pass it on. In this
they are poets as much as
the visitor who says,
Ohhh, a shooting star,
after she's been told
nothing is burning, nothing shooting,
merely molecules of sky jumping
as dust from beyond whizzes by.
Here is the world's biggest mirror –

a million dollars to cast
the glass in hexagonal molds,
to spin the gleaming saucer
parabolic, then a computer
to cool it cell by cell –
six weeks of that and then another
million, two years to polish
the surface to digital perfection.
Here are those gods and goddesses
seen for what they are – battered rock
and frigid gas, sulfur boiling out
into murderous air –
all of us here together
watching from our blue oasis,
whirling in a frozen fading night
where there is not enough
matter to explain why any of it
is here.

Consider the moon. A fault
visible tonight near the terminator
looks like a crease in fresh plaster.
Sea of Rains, Ocean of Storms.
But it has never been moist,
never felt dew or rivers.
Marsh of Sleep, Sea of Ingenuity –
a map of our misunderstanding.
The wonder is we still can see
the way it pours liquid pearl
over the earth's dark waters
after we know its windless surface,
that implacable dust the moon travelers said
smelled like cap guns, is cratered
with a wire-braced flag, two lunar jeeps,
and footprints no weather will arrive to erase.

Here is the observatory at 1 a.m.,
white domes humming on the mountain top
like brains, antennae feeling
(a mechanism wired) their way
into the wilderness. They won't explain
a thing about the wealth
of blackberries in Labrador,
or the sleep of velvet bats
hanging in the eaves drugged by the sun.
They won't fix history or touch the places
inside we can't get close to.
Looking up, we just keep falling.
Here are the owls who navigate
in darkness, here the scattered prey.

GEOFFREY LEHMANN

The Golden Wall

Don't ask Uncle Pat why the night sky is dark –
in hot weather
taking his mattress out on the grass
inside his dog-proof fence to sleep.
When Pat lifts his face up to the night –
propped on a pillow
of kapok stuffed in mattress ticking –
he'd fix you with sheep drench if you told him
that his line of sight
should intersect at every point
with a near or distant star
glimmering in the transparency of space
so the whole sky
should be ablaze from end to end
like 'a golden wall'.
Pat's golden wall was his orange tree.
Like Uncle Pat it had never borne fruit
until I dumped five tons of chicken manure
on its roots.
His line of sight
from the cane lounge where he sprawled
intersected at every point with oranges
twenty feet up in the sky,
a Utopia of fruit
which the district came to visit and eat,
oranges with no ending
like the return veranda
around the four sides of his house
where nephews and nieces ran forever
and their children after them.

Pat forgot his promise to pay for the manure
and the oranges didn't come back.
But he didn't miss them,
so don't ask Pat why the night sky is dark.

Olbers' riddle has hung around
for centuries.
You can't explain it by absorption.
Gas and dust heat up and glow.
Nor by absences or voids.
Every square inch has its galaxies.

Ask the cells inside your head
the same riddle,
why don't they all blaze at once
a golden wall of noise,
each neuron singing its own note
deafening your mind with light.
Political and religious visionaries
promise us this,
every cell singing in unison,
a mass of indistinguishable stars.

But something in the universe denies
the golden wall,
some structure which became Uncle Pat
calling to his nephews from his cane lounge,
'Now don't trample down them tomahawk plants!'
(meaning hollyhock plants).

Pat prefers his own company on hot nights
leaving Auntie Bridge inside
with pictures of saints on the bedroom wall.

He takes his bedding
and lies in a darkness
where each star can broadcast as a soloist.

The universe
is a composition of unique bodies
on display,
and the night sky of the mind
allows a single file of thoughts
to light up as a sentence.

The Song of the Happy Shepherd

The woods of Arcady are dead,
And over is their antique joy;
Of old the world on dreaming fed;
Grey Truth is now her painted toy;
Yet still she turns her restless head:
But O, sick children of the world,
Of all the many changing things
In dreary dancing past us whirled,
To the cracked tune that Chronos sings,
Words alone are certain good.
Where are now the warring kings,
Word be-mockers? – By the Rood
Where are now the warring kings?
An idle word is now their glory,
By the stammering schoolboy said,
Reading some entangled story:
The kings of the old time are dead;
The wandering earth herself may be
Only a sudden flaming word,
In clanging space a moment heard,
Troubling the endless reverie.

Then nowise worship dusty deeds,
Nor seek, for this is also sooth,
To hunger fiercely after truth,
Lest all thy toiling only breeds
New dreams, new dreams; there is no truth
Saving in thine own heart. Seek then,
No learning from the starry men
Who follow with the optic glass

The whirling ways of stars that pass –
Seek, then, for this is also sooth,
No words of theirs – the cold star-bane
Has cloven and rent their hearts in twain,
And dead is all their human truth.
Go gather by the humming sea
Some twisted, echo-harbouring shell,
And to its lips thy story tell,
And they thy comforters will be,
Rewarding in melodious guile
Thy fretful words a little while,
Till they shall singing fade in ruth
And die a pearly brotherhood;
For words alone are certain good:
Sing, then, for this is also sooth.

I must be gone: there is a grave
Where daffodil and lily wave,
And I would please the hapless faun,
Buried under the sleepy ground,
With mirthful songs before the dawn.
His shouting days with mirth were crowned;
And still I dream he treads the lawn,
Walking ghostly in the dew,
Pierced by my glad singing through,
My songs of old earth's dreamy youth:
But ah! she dreams not now; dream thou!
For fair are poppies on the brow:
Dream, dream, for this is also sooth.

NEIL ROLLINSON

The Very Small Baseline Group Convenes at the Cat and Fiddle

A groaning table of empties makes up
our Very Small Array – a barley-scented
interferometer. Here we can study the cosmos
and drink. We tune in to the microwave sky:
to the froth at the edge of the universe.
We sup in the dusk, everything glows
with its own light: the hedgerow, lawn,
the atoms inside the glass. The Milky Way
sings in a half-inch of Guinness
a song of the distant past when the world
was a moment old. We gather it all in our mugs,
in a pub garden on the edge of the moors,
looking down on Jodrell Bank: Queen
of the red-light district, cocking her huge lug
to the mayhem beyond our patch.
The bats are in on it, hunting in ultrasound,
catching moths in their fangs, while frogs
bark in the meadows, one to the other,
a vast unfathomable love-song. I finish my pint
and add my glass to the phalanx: the more we drink
the clearer we see, as any old soak will tell you.
I tip back my head to look at the Pleiades
and tumble, arse over tit, into the damp grass.
I lie in my cups under the bling of the northern sky.
I can hear it now, I can see it all clearly,
all and nothing, just the whole sky blazing.

FLEUR ADCOCK

The Ex-queen
among the Astronomers

They serve revolving saucer eyes,
dishes of stars; they wait upon
huge lenses hung aloft to frame
the slow procession of the skies.

They calculate, adjust, record,
watch transits, measure distances.
They carry pocket telescopes
to spy through when they walk abroad.

Spectra possess their eyes; they face
upwards, alert for meteorites,
cherishing little glassy worlds:
receptacles for outer space.

But she, exile, expelled, ex-queen,
swishes among the men of science
waiting for cloudy skies, for nights
when constellations can't be seen.

She wears the rings he let her keep;
she walks as she was taught to walk
for his approval, years ago.
His bitter features taunt her sleep.

And so when these have laid aside
their telescopes, when lids are closed

between machine and sky, she seeks
terrestrial bodies to bestride.

She plucks this one or that among
the astronomers, and is become
his canopy, his occultation;
she sucks at earlobe, penis, tongue

mouthing the tubes of flesh; her hair
crackles, her eyes are comet-sparks.
She brings the distant briefly close
above his dreamy abstract stare.

Star-Gazer

The very stars are justified.
The galaxy
italicized.

I have proofread
and proofread
the beautiful script.

There are no
errors.

WALT WHITMAN

When I Heard the Learn'd Astronomer

When I heard the learn'd astronomer,
When the proofs, the figures, were ranged in columns before me,
When I was shown the charts and diagrams, to add, divide,
   and measure them,
When I sitting heard the astronomer where he lectured with
   much applause in the lecture-room,
How soon unaccountable I became tired and sick,
Till rising and gliding out I wander'd off by myself,
In the mystical moist night-air, and from time to time,
Look'd up in perfect silence at the stars.

STANLEY KUNITZ

The Science of the Night

I touch you in the night, whose gift was you,
My careless sprawler,
And I touch you cold, unstirring, star-bemused,
That are become the land of your self-strangeness.
What long seduction of the bone has led you
Down the imploring roads I cannot take
Into the arms of ghosts I never knew,
Leaving my manhood on a rumpled field
To guard you where you lie so deep
In absent-mindedness,
Caught in the calcium snows of sleep?

And even should I track you to your birth
Through all the cities of your mortal trial,
As in my jealous thought I try to do,
You would escape me – from the brink of earth
Take off to where the lawless auroras run,
You with your wild and metaphysic heart.
My touch is on you, who are light-years gone.
We are not souls but systems, and we move
In clouds of our unknowing
                              like great nebulae.
Our very motives swirl and have their start
With father lion and with mother crab.

Dreamer, my own lost rib,
Whose planetary dust is blowing
Past archipelagoes of myth and light,
What far Magellans are you mistress of
To whom you speed the pleasure of your art?

As through a glass that magnifies my loss
I see the lines of your spectrum shifting red,
The universe expanding, thinning out,
Our worlds flying, oh flying, fast apart.

From hooded powers and from abstract flight
I summon you, your person and your pride.
Fall to me now from outer space,
Still fastened desperately to my side;
Through gulfs of streaming air
Bring me the mornings of the milky ways
Down to my threshold in your drowsy eyes;
And by the virtue of your honeyed word
Restore the liquid language of the moon,
That in gold mines of secrecy you delve.
Awake!
       My whirling hands stay at the noon,
Each cell within my body holds a heart
And all my hearts in unison strike twelve.

ALAN DUGAN

Prothalamion of Quantum Mechanics and Astrophysics

Against the Text *Philosophia Biou Kubernetes* (Philosophy the Guide of Life)

Part I: The Stutter of Quanta

It is impossible. The Uncertainty Principle
is Planck's Constant, 6.624 (or 5) times 10^{-27}
divided by two pis or more, more.
It is ridiculous, I am approximate,
we are either always flying apart and getting larger
or getting too close together in too small a way.
The intrusion of my gross instrument
distorts my knowledge of exactly
where you're at, you are so moving,
of exactly how you're moving where you're at.
Oh I can know your position but not
your velocity, your velocity but not your position,
and your position changes every time you make a motion.
You have to make a motion to take a position in this matter
and your position changes every time
you make a motion and your motions change,
and you are always taking up positions on my instrument
and making motions. I think
that you turn on and off.
You turn me off and on.
You part your wave
and wave your thing
at me.

You part your thing
at me
and wave your part.

You part your part
and wave your wave
at me.
You wave and part
and part and wave
your thing and part,
waving,

         at me.

I withdraw inconsummate
if you are approximate,
I am empty, I
am in val-
id, I represent no
knowable abstraction if
I love you only because
you have no definite figure.
My love is incomplete in theory.
My love is uncertain in principle.
Whether you matter or
do not matter, whether
you are real or false,
I either love or am the law.
Therefore I will be as constant
as Max Planck's Constant is constant,
though divided in this farce
by two pis or more, more.

Part II: Dirge/Scherzo

                    In dreams I think
                    you are behaving like
                    my model universe
but know that you're
not sensible and that
you have a cloudy past,
no definite figure,
and are infinitely multiple,
divisible eternally,
but you are everything to me
so I want all of you
to be (Please be)
(considered as) my only one,
I want all of you
to be my only one.

What can I say as we go away
from one another, you and I,
except that I am not thoughtful,
that I am insensitive and imperceptive.
I don't even know if I could hope
that you and I could get together again,
or else slow down and find stability,
or simply go away forever, fast,
and leave me saying empty verse
out to an emptying universe:

        Oh I don't know where you're going,
I don't know where you're at.
I don't know where you come from
or if you're coming back,
so tell me how I love you.

Part III: Antennae of Astrophysics and The End of Optics

I hear you after I see your light
and see you after I feel your stroke.
How you come on and then go off
without a sound, and then the sound
sounds. What struck me first,
and in the afterlight, and then,
when the noise came later, was
that touch, sounds and lights
must move at various speeds,
but speeds, and light is slow, slow:
we never see each other now,
but see each other either long
or just a little while ago,

so we live in one another's pasts,
you and I, and go into our own
futures all alone. We are always
moving apart and getting larger
and looking smaller, you in your
beautiful red shift, and me,
bug-eyed, observatory, shelled,
waving my antennae out at you
and flying away. I have my doubts
that I'm your metamorphic worm,
yolked in your egg of unknowability
and flying timewise to be born or burned.

ANTJIE KROG

I Am, Because You Are*

*Axiom of African Philosophy emphasizing the interconnectedness of everything

1.
what sense does the down on your cheek make
as gravity crunches ice-stone and dust
collisions leave debris and flaring hot kernels
devouring moons, tearing up small stars, pulverizing surfaces
as swarms of stars scrounge on cloud-ice and gleaming gas-jets?

why would your left cheek come to mind
surrounded as we are by scorching balls
helium, sun winds, impact craters
and gravitation whirlpools where giant stars implode so forcibly
that not even light escapes?

among left-behind-wells of darkness
black holes where nothing but violence holds forth
what is the use of a tender gesture?

if solar systems shoot apart as if hurled in fury
driven by consuming temperatures and unknowable speeds
if a centre-less universe fills all space
by making space where space never was space
if unseen, unsaid dark matter
threatens to blot out fragmentary haloes and the few scribblings
    of light
then my thumb tracing your lower lip has no place

2.

but spiral arms exist, you say
the lovely, feathery, slender spiral arms of our galaxy exist
in a dreamlike ballet, you say, of nebulae and orbits
and the slow pulsing lifespan of stars
spiral arms exist, you say, and oxygen and quasars
and nebulous uteruses from which protostars stumble dizzily
whirlpools, nebulae and star-heaps exist
quasars exist, stable gravity exists
and immense luminosity from the outskirts of the visible universe,
you say spiral arms exist, the Milky Way exists
smooth orbits exist, the lovable-ness of moons
tides exist and eternal equilibrium, all of these exist, you say

but it is the stars as piercings of light on a summer evening
that keep us in orbits of reaching out
every time we turn towards each other
we do it under a sweeping baldachin of stars

3. Symmetry *(HH 212)*

At first, you do not see the edge-on disk's accreting might
  twirling out gas jets into opposite directions –
   both of them pulsing luminous squirts in tight
    semi-benign collusions, bump-bumping,
     egging each other into sight: see how
      within her cleaving elbows, the star now threads
       on either side, delicately, incandescent vertebrae of light.
       On either side, delicately, incandescent vertebrae of light
      within her cleaving elbows, the star now threads
     egging them into sight: see how
    semi-benign collusions, bump-bumping
   both of them pulsing luminous squirts in tight
  twirling gas jets in opposite directions –
at first, you do not see the edge-on disk's accreting might.

4.

through your body I understand the pockmarked Mercury
with its powdery seas and centre of iron

through your body I weather the sun wind from Venus
the inferno of it, the orange sky, the biting verdigris
and its slow-slow twirling – to the other side

through your body I embrace Earth
waterplanet spinning within light fingerprints of vapour

through your body I plough duststorms from Mars
ochre, frosted, sulphur-stained, desert planet
measuring its two tiny captured moons

through your body the enormity of Jupiter overwhelms me
the mighty speed, that circulating red-infested abscess
the mass of moons as creamy lanes, smoky fluttering patterns
and metal tints guide its girth

through your body I adore exquisite Saturn
the quiet yellow light, the captive caressing of rings
the spaces between the rings, the smoothness thereof
the exuberance of a perfect form and the elegant angle of its tilt
so light are you Saturn, you can float on water

through your body I stare at the pearl eye of Uranus
fallen on its side, fallen, heavy with methane and soundless song

through your body I find blue dark Neptune
mumbling under gas-oceans, hidden, morose, chilled
in a never-ending west wind at the furthest edges of solar gloom

only through your mortal and bony body, beloved
– my tuning fork to the skies –
can I crash in terror and ecstasy into the time and the space of stars

(oh dearest, your cheek waxing in my palm, the wounding
forgive me the wounding

THOMAS HARDY

The Comet at Yell'ham

It bends far over Yell'ham Plain,
   And we, from Yell'ham Height,
Stand and regard its fiery train,
   So soon to swim from sight.

It will return long years hence, when
   As now its strange swift shine
Will fall on Yell'ham; but not then
   On that sweet form of thine.

Halley's Comet

Miss Murphy in first grade
wrote its name in chalk
across the board and told us
it was roaring down the stormtracks
of the Milky Way at frightful speed
and if it wandered off its course
and smashed into the earth
there'd be no school tomorrow.
A red-bearded preacher from the hills
with a wild look in his eyes
stood in the public square
at the playground's edge
proclaiming he was sent by God
to save every one of us,
even the little children.
'Repent, ye sinners!' he shouted,
waving his hand-lettered sign.
At supper I felt sad to think
that it was probably
the last meal I'd share
with my mother and sisters;
but I felt excited too
and scarcely touched my plate.
So mother scolded me
and sent me early to my room.
The whole family's asleep
except for me. They never heard me steal
into the stairwell hall and climb
the ladder to the fresh night air.
Look for me, Father, on the roof

of the red brick building
at the foot of Green Street –
that's where we live, you know, on the top floor.
I'm the boy in the white flannel gown
sprawled on this coarse gravel bed
searching the starry sky,
waiting for the world to end.

GWYNETH LEWIS

from Zero Gravity

V

First time I saw the comet, I finally knew
That I'd always love him. I watched it go,

dead starlight headed for a dying sun
then away into darkness. It was gone

before we knew what its brilliance meant,
a human moment in immense

spirals of nothing. I feel his pull
in my blood salts. The comet's tail

is a searchlight from another point,
and the point is once you've given your heart

there are no replacements. Oh, your soul,
if that can escape from its own black hole.

XI

The second time the comet swung by
the knife went deeper. It hissed through the sky

like phosphorus on water. It marked a now,
an only-coming-once, a this-ness we knew

we'd keep forgetting. Its vapour trails
mimicked our voyage along ourselves,

our fire with each other, the endless cold
which surrounds that burning. Don't be fooled

by fireworks. It's no accident that *leave*
fails but still tries to rhyme with *love*.

XV
Last sight of the comet. The sky's a screen
riddled with pinpricks, hung in between

me and what happened – a room not quite
hidden from me. Hale-Bopp's light

says something dazzling's taking place beyond,
involving moving. My mind

is silver nitrate, greedy for form
but I fail to grasp it here in this gloom.

Memory's a crude camera.
I wish you were seared on my retina

so I was blind to anything less
than your leaving. But the darkness

is kind. Dawn will heal with colour
my grief for your self-consuming core.

SEAMUS HEANEY

Exposure

It is December in Wicklow:
Alders dripping, birches
Inheriting the last light,
The ash tree cold to look at.

A comet that was lost
Should be visible at sunset,
Those million tons of light
Like a glimmer of haws and rose-hips,

And I sometimes see a falling star.
If I could come on meteorite!
Instead I walk through damp leaves,
Husks, the spent flukes of autumn,

Imagining a hero
On some muddy compound,
His gift like a slingstone
Whirled for the desperate.

How did I end up like this?
I often think of my friends'
Beautiful, prismatic counselling
And the anvil brains of some who hate me

As I sit weighing and weighing
My responsible *tristia*.
For what? For the ear? For the people?
For what is said behind-backs?

Rain comes down through the alders,
Its low conducive voices
Mutter about let-downs and erosions
And yet each drop recalls

The diamond absolutes.
I am neither internee nor informer;
An inner émigré, grown long-haired
And thoughtful; a wood-kerne

Escaped from the massacre,
Taking protective colouring
From bole and bark, feeling
Every wind that blows;

Who, blowing up these sparks
For their meagre heat, have missed
The once-in-a-lifetime portent,
The comet's pulsing rose.

JAMES THOMSON

from The Seasons

[Night. Summer Meteors. A Comet]

   Among the crooked lanes, on every hedge,
The glow-worm lights his gem; and, through the dark,
A moving radiance twinkles. Evening yields
The world to Night; not in her winter robe
Of massy Stygian woof, but loose arrayed
In mantle dun. A faint erroneous ray,
Glanced from the imperfect surfaces of things,
Flings half an image on the straining eye;
While wavering woods, and villages, and streams,
And rocks, and mountain-tops that long retained
The ascending gleam are all one swimming scene,
Uncertain if beheld. Sudden to heaven
Thence weary vision turns; where, leading soft
The silent hours of love, with purest ray
Sweet Venus shines; and, from her genial rise,
When daylight sickens, till it springs afresh,
Unrivalled reigns, the fairest lamp of night.
As thus the effulgence tremulous I drink,
With cherished gaze, the lambent lightnings shoot
Across the sky, or horizontal dart
In wondrous shapes – by fearful murmuring crowds
Portentous deemed. Amid the radiant orbs
That more than deck, that animate the sky,
The life-infusing suns of other worlds,
Lo! from the dread immensity of space
Returning with accelerated course,
The rushing comet to the sun descends;
And, as he sinks below the shading earth,

With awful train projected o'er the heavens,
The guilty nations tremble. But, above
Those superstitious horrors that enslave
The fond sequacious herd, to mystic faith
And blind amazement prone, the enlightened few,
Whose godlike minds philosophy exalts,
The glorious stranger hail. They feel a joy
Divinely great; they in their powers exult,
That wondrous force of thought, which mounting spurns
This dusky spot, and measures all the sky;
While, from his far excursion through the wilds
Of barren ether, faithful to his time,
They see the blazing wonder rise anew,
In seeming terror clad, but kindly bent,
To work the will of all-sustaining love –
From his huge vapoury train perhaps to shake
Reviving moisture on the numerous orbs
Through which his long ellipsis winds, perhaps
To lend new fuel to declining suns,
To light up worlds, and feed the eternal fire.

IAIN CRICHTON SMITH

'Tinily a Star Goes Down'

Tinily a star goes down
behind a black cloud.

Odd that your wristwatch still should lie
on the shiny dressing table

its tick so faint I cannot hear
the universe at its centre.

LOUIS MacNEICE

Star-gazer

Forty-two years ago (to me if to no one else
The number is of some interest) it was a brilliant starry night
And the westward train was empty and had no corridors
So darting from side to side I could catch the unwonted sight
Of those almost intolerably bright
Holes, punched in the sky, which excited me partly because
Of their Latin names and partly because I had read in the textbooks
How very far off they were, it seemed their light
Had left them (some at least) long years before I was.

And this remembering now I mark that what
Light was leaving some of them at least then,
Forty-two years ago, will never arrive
In time for me to catch it, which light when
It does get here may find that there is not
Anyone left alive
To run from side to side in a late night train
Admiring it and adding noughts in vain.

Star-Gazers

What crowd is this? what have we here! we must not pass it by;
A Telescope upon its frame, and pointed to the sky:
Long is it as a barber's pole, or mast of little boat,
Some little pleasure-skiff, that doth on Thames's waters float.

The Showman chooses well his place, 'tis Leicester's busy Square;
And is as happy in his night, for the heavens are blue and fair;
Calm, though impatient, is the crowd; each stands ready with the fee,
And envies him that's looking; – what an insight must it be!

Yet, Showman, where can lie the cause? Shall thy Implement
   have blame,
A boaster that, when he is tried, fails, and is put to shame?
Or is it good as others are, and be their eyes in fault?
Their eyes, or minds? or, finally, is yon resplendent vault?

Is nothing of that radiant pomp so good as we have here?
Or gives a thing but small delight that never can be dear?
The silver moon with all her vales, and hills of mightiest fame,
Doth she betray us when they're seen? or are they but a name?

Or is it rather that Conceit rapacious is and strong,
And bounty never yields so much but it seems to do her wrong?
Or is it that, when human Souls a journey long have had
And are returned into themselves, they cannot but be sad?

Or must we be constrained to think that these Spectators rude,
Poor in estate, of manners base, men of the multitude,
Have souls which never yet have risen, and therefore prostrate lie?
No, no, this cannot be; – men thirst for power and majesty!

Does, then, a deep and earnest thought the blissful mind employ
Of him who gazes, or has gazed? a grave and steady joy,
That doth reject all show of pride, admits no outward sign,
Because not of this noisy world, but silent and divine!

Whatever be the cause, 'tis sure that they who pry and pore
Seem to meet with little gain, seem less happy than before:
One after One they take their turn, nor have I one espied
That doth not slackly go away, as if dissatisfied.

ELIZABETH JENNINGS

Stargazers and Others

One, staring out stars,
Lost himself in looking and almost
Forgot glass, eye, air, space;
Simply, he thought, the world is improved
By my staring, how the still glass leaps
When the sky thuds in like tides.

Another, making love, once
Stared so far over his pleasure
That woman, world, the spiral
Of taut bodies, the clinging hands, broke apart
And he saw, as the stargazer sees,
Landscapes made to be looked at,
Fruit to fall, not be plucked.

In you also something
Of such vision occurs.
How else would I have learnt
The tapered stars, the pause
On the nervous spiral? Names I need
Stronger than love, desire,
Passion, pleasure. O discover
Some star and christen it, but let me be
The space that your eye moves over.

GEORGE HERBERT

The Starre

Bright spark, shot from a brighter place,
　Where beams surround my Saviours face,
　　　Canst thou be any where
　　　　So well as there?

Yet, if thou wilt from thence depart,
　Take a bad lodging in my heart;
　　　For thou canst make a debter,
　　　　And make it better.

First with thy fire-work burn to dust
　Folly, and worse then folly, lust:
　　　Then with thy light refine,
　　　　And make it shine:

So disengag'd from sinne and sicknesse,
　Touch it with thy celestiall quicknesse,
　　　That it may hang and move
　　　　After thy love.

Then with our trinitie of light,
　Motion, and heat, let's take our flight
　　　Unto the place where thou
　　　　Before didst bow.

Get me a standing there, and place
　Among the beams, which crown the face
　　　Of him, who dy'd to part
　　　　Sinne and my heart:

That so among the rest I may
   Glitter, and curle, and winde as they:
      That winding is their fashion
        Of adoration.

Sure thou wilt joy, by gaining me
   To flie home like a laden bee
      Unto that hive of beams
        And garland-streams.

JOHN KEATS

'Bright Star, Would I Were Steadfast as Thou Art'

Bright star, would I were steadfast as thou art –
Not in lone splendour hung aloft the night
And watching, with eternal lids apart,
Like nature's patient, sleepless eremite,
The moving waters at their priestlike task
Of pure ablution round earth's human shores,
Or gazing on the new soft-fallen mask
Of snow upon the mountains and the moors –
No – yet still steadfast, still unchangeable,
Pillow'd upon my fair love's ripening breast,
To feel for ever its soft fall and swell,
Awake for ever in a sweet unrest,
Still, still to hear her tender-taken breath,
And so live ever – or else swoon to death.

JOHN KINSELLA

The Light Echo of Supernova 1987A

after David Malin

Dust sheet to dust sheet, black stars
overlay lichenous surface, and shockwave
resonance, rings in the vacuum,
against granite. The map we go by,
touchpaper, bird's-eye view of birds,
eternally endstopped cosmos.
Today, examining blank spots

in the year's early green, post-April rains,
we searched the eye of logic. Empiricism.
Honestly, we waited for the expansive
corona to throw its lasso, light echo, so many days
lying on our sides, imprint and impound,
green edge stretching up-country. Where
it will never end, it ended, and still

unravelled. Surprisingly, none lay claim
to a spiritualism, none make contact
with an emanating dead; come back always
to the same spot, as if off-centre
new centres will be made. Inclusive,
haunting of entirety. But not so, nor a hazy
suspension of willingness to believe,

gravel, sand, clay, sprouts of wild oats,
Paterson's curse, castings of numerous
species of insects, an assortment of bark fibres,
beneath our feet. Contrary to sky,

to heavens. But not so, nor the bell chime
at the end of time, nor reverberations
through the valley. It's neither a day

nor a night thing. And we don't need to see
the artefact, the made moment to know
all moments are in there, mythic as speech,
as eating, as travel. Stock still, we sense,
or it senses us, spike to arrest rings
thrown out to fall down somewhere.
The birds that pursue whatever moves

suddenly, whatever is small enough
not to miss, large waves diluted out, or
are they? Probably not. Not even birds
from the continent's opposing edge,
collecting bits of blue, make statements
of belonging and ownership. We say
they do but they don't. Epicentres
of vastness, seeds of outburst, like us.

WILLIAM BLAKE

To the Evening Star

Thou fair-hair'd angel of the evening,
Now, while the sun rests on the mountains, light
Thy bright torch of love; thy radiant crown
Put on, and smile upon our evening bed!
Smile on our loves; and, while thou drawest the
Blue curtains of the sky, scatter thy silver dew
On every flower that shuts its sweet eyes
In timely sleep. Let thy west wind sleep on
The lake; speak silence with thy glimmering eyes,
And wash the dusk with silver. Soon, full soon,
Dost thou withdraw; then the wolf rages wide,
And the lion glares thro' the dun forest:
The fleeces of our flocks are cover'd with
Thy sacred dew: protect them with thine influence.

PHILIP LEVINE

The Doctor of Starlight

'Show me the place,' he said.
I removed my shirt and pointed
to a tiny star above my heart.
He leaned and listened. I could feel
his breath falling lightly, flattening
the hairs on my chest. He turned
me around, and his hands gently
plied my shoulder blades and then rose
to knead the twin columns forming
my neck. 'You are an athlete?'
'No,' I said, 'I'm a working man.'
'And you make?' he said. 'I make
the glare for lightbulbs.' 'Yes,
where would we be without them?'
'In the dark.' I heard the starched
dress of the nurse behind me,
and then together they helped me
lie face up on his table, where blind
and helpless I thought of all
the men and women who had surrendered
and how little good it had done them.
The nurse took my right wrist
in both of her strong hands, and I
saw the doctor lean toward me,
a tiny chrome knife glinting in
one hand and tweezers in the other.
I could feel nothing, and then he said
proudly, 'I have it!' and held up
the perfect little blue star, no
longer me and now bloodless. 'And do

you know what we have under it?'
'No,' I said. 'Another perfect star.'
I closed my eyes, but the lights
still swam before me in a sea
of golden fire. 'What does it mean?'
'Mean?' he said, dabbing the place
with something cool and liquid,
and all the lights were blinking on
and off, or perhaps my eyes were
opening and closing. 'Mean?' he said,
'It could mean this is who you are.'

GEORGE MEREDITH

Lucifer in Starlight

On a starred night Prince Lucifer uprose.
Tired of his dark dominion swung the fiend
Above the rolling ball in cloud part screened,
Where sinners hugged their spectre of repose.
Poor prey to his hot fit of pride were those.
And now upon his western wing he leaned,
Now his huge bulk o'er Afric's sands careened,
Now the black planet shadowed Arctic snows.
Soaring through wider zones that pricked his scars
With memory of the old revolt from Awe,
He reached a middle height, and at the stars,
Which are the brain of heaven, he looked, and sank.
Around the ancient track marched, rank on rank,
The army of unalterable law.

JOHN MILTON

from Paradise Lost

Book 3, ll. 555–623

[Satan Visits the Sun]

Round he surveys, and well might, where he stood
So high above the circling canopy
Of night's extended shade; from eastern point
Of Libra to the fleecy star that bears
Andromeda far off Atlantic seas
Beyond th' horizon; then from pole to pole
He views in breadth, and without longer pause
Down right into the world's first region throws
His flight precipitant, and winds with ease
Through the pure marble air his oblique way
Amongst innumerable stars, that shone
Stars distant, but nigh hand seemed other worlds,
Or other worlds they seemed, or happy isles,
Like those Hesperian gardens famed of old,
Fortunate fields, and groves and flow'ry vales,
Thrice happy isles, but who dwelt happy there
He stayed not to inquire: above them all
The golden sun in splendor likest Heaven
Allured his eye: thither his course he bends
Through the calm firmament; but up or down
By center, or eccentric, hard to tell,
Or longitude, where the great luminary
Aloof the vulgar constellations thick,
That from his lordly eye keep distance due,
Dispenses light from far; they as they move
Their starry dance in numbers that compute

Days, months, and years, towards his all-cheering lamp
Turn swift their various motions, or are turned
By his magnetic beam, that gently warms
The universe, and to each inward part
With gentle penetration, though unseen,
Shoots invisible virtue even to the deep:
So wondrously was set his station bright.
There lands the fiend, a spot like which perhaps
Astronomer in the sun's lucent orb
Through his glazed optic tube yet never saw.
The place he found beyond expression bright,
Compared with aught on Earth, metal or stone;
Not all parts like, but all alike informed
With radiant light, as glowing iron with fire;
If metal, part seemed gold, part silver clear;
If stone, carbuncle most or chrysolite,
Ruby or topaz, to the twelve that shone
In Aaron's breastplate, and a stone besides
Imagined rather oft than elsewhere seen,
That stone, or like to that which here below
Philosophers in vain so long have sought,
In vain, though by their powerful art they bind
Volatile Hermes, and call up unbound
In various shapes old Proteus from the sea,
Drained through a limbec to his native form.
What wonder then if fields and regions here
Breathe forth elixir pure, and rivers run
Potable gold, when with one virtuous touch
Th' arch-chemic sun so far from us remote
Produces with terrestrial humor mixed
Here in the dark so many precious things
Of color glorious and effect so rare?
Here matter new to gaze the Devil met
Undazzled, far and wide his eye commands,
For sight no obstacle found here, nor shade,

But all sunshine, as when his beams at noon
Culminate from th'equator, as they now
Shot upward still direct, whence no way round
Shadow from body opaque can fall, and the air,
Nowhere so clear, sharpened his visual ray
To objects distant far, whereby he soon
Saw within ken a glorious angel stand,
The same whom John saw also in the sun ...

ANNA LAETITIA BARBAULD

from A Summer Evening's Meditation

                              Seiz'd in thought
On fancy's wild and roving wing I sail,
From the green borders of the peopled earth,
And the pale moon, her duteous fair attendant;
From solitary Mars; from the vast orb
Of Jupiter, whose huge gigantic bulk
Dances in ether like the lightest leaf;
To the dim verge, the suburbs of the system,
Where chearless Saturn 'midst her watry moons
Girt with a lucid zone, majestic sits
In gloomy grandeur; like an exil'd queen
Amongst her weeping handmaids: fearless thence
I launch into the trackless deeps of space,
Where, burning round, ten thousand suns appear,
Of elder beam; which ask no leave to shine
Of our terrestrial star, nor borrow light
From the proud regent of our scanty day;
Sons of the morning, first born of creation,
And only less than him who marks their track,
And guides their fiery wheels. Here must I stop,
Or is there aught beyond? What hand unseen
Impels me onward thro' the glowing orbs
Of habitable nature; far remote,
To the dread confines of eternal night,
To solitudes of vast unpeopled space,
The desarts of creation, wide and wild;
Where embryo systems and unkindled suns
Sleep in the womb of chaos; fancy droops,
And thought astonish'd stops her bold career.

ALICE OSWALD

Excursion to the Planet Mercury

certain evenings a little before the golden
foam of the horizon has properly hardened
you can see a tiny iron island
very close indeed to the sun.

all craters and mirrors, the uncanny country
of the planet Mercury – a mystery
without I without air,
without you without sound.

in that violently magic little place
the sky is racing along
like a blue wrapper flapped and let go
from a car window.

now hot now cold
the ground moves fast,
a few stones frisk about
looking for a foothold

but it shales it slides
the whole concept is only
loosely fastened
to a few tweaks of gravity.

o the weather is dreadful there:
thousand-year showers of dust
all dandruff and discarded shells
of creatures too swift to exist:

paupers beggars toughs
boys in dresses
who come alive and crumble
at the mercy or metamorphosis.

no nothing accumulates there
not even mist
nothing but glimmering beginnings
making ready to manifest.

as for the catastrophe
of nights on mercury,
hiding in a rock-smashed hollow
at about two hundred degrees below zero

the feather-footed winds
take off their guises there,
they go in gym shoes
thieving and lifting

and their amazed expressions
have been soundproofed, nevertheless
they go on howling
for gladness sheer gladness

from Ariosto's Orlando Furioso,
in English Heroical Verse

[Astolfo flies by Chariot to the Moon,
where he collects Orlando's lost wits]

I say although the fire were wondrous hot,
    Yet in their passage they no heat did feele,
    So that it burnd them, nor offends them not;
    Thence to the moone he guids the running wheele,
    The Moone was like a glasse all voyd of spot,
    Or like a peece of purelie burnisht steele,
    And lookt, although to us it seems so small,
    Well nye as bigg as earth, and sea and all.

Here had *Astolfo* cause of double wonder,
    One, that that region seemeth there so wyde,
    That unto us that are so far a sunder,
    Seems but a little circle, and beside,
    That to behold the ground that him lay under,
    A man had need to have been sharply eyd,
    And bend his brows, and marke ev'n all they might,
    It seemed so small, now chiefly wanting light.

Twere infinit to tell what wondrous things
    He saw, that passed ours not few degrees,
    What towns, what hills, what rivers and what springs,
    What dales, what Pallaces, what goodly trees:
    But to be short, at last his guide him brings,
    Unto a goodlie vallie, where he sees,
    A mightie masse of things straungely confused,
    Things that on earth were lost, or were abused.

A store house straunge, that what on earth is lost,
    By fault, by time, by fortune, there is found,
    And like a marchaundise is there engrost,
    In straunger sort then I can well expound:
    Nor speake I sole of wealth, or things of cost,
    In which blind fortunes powre doth most abound,
    But ev'n of things quite out of fortunes powre,
    Which wilfullie we wast each day and houre.

The precious time that fools mispend in play,
    The vaine attempts that never take effect,
    The vows that sinners make, and never pay,
    The counsells wise that carelesse men neglect,
    The fond desires that lead us oft astray,
    The prayses that with pride the heart infect,
    And all we loose with follie and mispending,
    May there be found unto this place ascending.

Now, as *Astolfo* by those regions past,
    He asked many questions of his guide,
    And as he on t'one side his eye did cast,
    A wondrous hill of bladders he espyde;
    And he was told they had been in time past,
    The pompous crowns and scepters, full of pride,
    Of Monarks of Assiria, and of Greece,
    Of which now scantlie there is left a peece.

He saw great store of baited hookes with gold,
    And those were gifts that foolish men prepard,
    To give to Princes covetous and old,
    With fondest hope of future vaine reward:
    Then were there ropes all in sweet garlands rold,
    And those were all false flatteries he hard,
    Then hard he crickets songs like to the verses,
    The servant in his masters prayse reherses.

There did he see fond loves, that men pursew,
    To looke like golden gyves with stones all set,
    Then things like Eagles talents he did vew,
    Those offices that favorites do get:
    Then saw he bellows large that much winde blew,
    Large promises that Lords make, and forget,
    Unto their Ganimeds in flowre of youth,
    But after nought but beggerie insewth.

He saw great Cities seated in fayre places,
    That overthrown quite topsie turvie stood,
    He askt and learnd, the cause of their defaces
    Was treason, that doth never turne to good:
    He saw fowle serpents, with fayre womens faces,
    Of coyners and of thieves the cursed brood,
    He saw fine glasses, all in peeces broken,
    Of service lost in court, a wofull token.

Of mingled broth he saw a mightie masse,
    That to no use, all spilt on ground did lye,
    He askt his teacher, and he heard it was,
    The fruitlesse almes that men geve when they dye:
    Then by a fayre green mountain he did passe,
    That once smelt sweet, but now it stinks perdye,
    This was the gift (be't said without offence)
    That *Constantin* gave *Silvester* long since.

Of birdlymd rodds, he saw no little store,
    And these (O Ladies fayre) your bewties be,
    I do omit ten thousand things and more
    Like unto these, that there the Duke did see
    For all that here is lost, there evermore
    Is kept, and thither in a trise doth flee,
    Howbeit more nor lesse there was no folly,
    For still that here with us remaineth wholly.

He saw some of his own lost time and deeds,
    But yet he knew them not to be his own,
    They seemed to him disguisd in so straunge weeds,
    Till his instructer made them better known:
    But last, the thing which no man thinks he needs,
    Yet each man needeth most, to him was shown,
    By name mans wit, which here we leese so fast,
    As that one substance, all the other past.

It seemd to be a body moyst and soft,
    And apt to mount by ev'ry exhalation,
    And when it hither mounted was aloft,
    It there was kept in potts of such a fashion,
    As we call Jarrs, where oyle is kept in oft:
    The Duke beheld with no small admiration,
    The Jarrs of wit, amongst which one had writ,
    Upon the side thereof, *Orlandos wit*.

JOHN HARTLEY WILLIAMS

from Dan Dare at the Cosmos Ballroom

amor vincit omnia

(i)
Venus lies ahead –
ball of mists and disenchanted fruitfulness,
too hot for charity, too steamy for reproach,
my mission crystalline as snow:
to conquer what has always conquered us.
Airlock doors slide open. They reveal
the Mekon, president of Love Unexpurgated,
a peagreen Humpty Dumpty on a flying plate,
vestigial legs suggesting
toxic misadventures at the ante-natal stage,
the sonic scalpel of his voice
sharp inside my brain: *Welcome to the planet*
humans dream of on their cold blue ball.
Welcome to the temperature of pleasant being.
Dispel colonial ideas.
We've been watching humans from afar.
How could anyone invent a game like cricket?
An egg-sliced-open sort of smile.
I descend the ladder of the **Peril Two**,
alight upon the sighing ground
and contemplate across the rocket park
The Cosmos Ballroom, with its astral sign:
Pleasure Tourist Amorous Infinity is Yours
Without Regards to Species, Origin, or Sex!
'Unappeasable amour?' I ask. 'Is that your creed?'
No, no, the Mekon says. *Creed is what Venusians*

have never suffered from. We give no credence anywhere.
He loops a solipsistic loop. Even upside
down his saucer holds him firmly glued:
Venusians adhere – I use the word advisedly –
to two adjacent modes of love,
PARADISE – he points to entrance Number One –
or its counterpart: DISASTER.
'No human,' I remark, 'would go through *that* door.'
Ah, the blindness of the Earthling, the Mekon says,
disaster if experienced aright
can be as pleasurable, indeed it may be more so,
than any mere paradise, whose quality…
and here the Mekon banks away, then comes zipping back,
… contains a level of inherent boredom
most Venusians, at least, deplore.
I jut my famous chin. Perhaps a man
of my renown should take disaster's door
to prove I'm up to it. This is Venus, after all.
My orders are to let the worst befall.
The Mekon has decided for me.
He nudges me with little bumps toward
a beckoning entrance, finger-fronded.
Through music that has fingers too,
notes that tweak my nose, and fidget
at the spaceworld issue of my pants,
tickled by the shadow of desire, or
seething with imperative, I go:
Now put on rollerblades,
slot them in this rail that weaves
a roller coaster tangle
over Consummation Chasm.
Keep your wits and balance, Dan Dare!
Lose your equilibrium, you'll fall,
and falling here on Venus is an endless process
that never stops… Suddenly,

I'm launched upon a steepening helter-skelter
in knee-alarming corkscrews.
Massed choirs keen from nowhere
JOIN US! JOIN US NOW DAN DARE!
The tracks I'm on keep branching. I derail.
A thousand million voices rise in song
to greet the imminence of my demise.
I lose my spaceworld cap.
My hair's a streak of flying sweat.
Wafting from the nether world
the limpid ditty fans me with its coo.
Skates jammed firmly back on track,
high above the lullabying tomb,
I bend my knees to take another curve.
A fiery catherine wheel displays:
ENTER THE ARCADIAN MAZE.
Here each decision, counting down, leaves more.
I swerve. The signs read
NO WAY OUT, NONE LEFT, NONE LEFT.
More decisions, all of them superfluous.
The false deliverance of an EXIT looms.
Go right? Go left?
I exit into more decisions.
Can this one be the FINAL EXIT?
And then another one. And billions more.
Switch. Turn. Twist. Dodge.
I'm going right. Then left. Then right again.
From vertigo, the chorusing abyss
reiterates its roundelay of little death:
La-la again. La-la again. La-la again.
Then I'm gliding to the station where the Mekon waits:
I thought the famished roar went up
that would have signified
your transmutation to a morsel of amor.
Well, well. They'll get their chance.

Nothing here, Dan Dare, that's not discoverable
from one fissipating body to the next…
Let's say this was
a little fitness test to get you in the mood for proper love…?
May I suggest a cup of sweet green tea?

LEO AYLEN

Orbiting Pluto

*An astronaut on the first manned expedition into deep space, on course
for the nearest planet where there might be life, orbits Pluto and its
moon, Charon, before leaving the solar system, and going into frozen
sleep for a journey of light years.*

A moon. But sixty times the size
Of ours. A faintly glimmering face,
Unchanging. Ice. Only this ice.
Dawn, but as frail as a weak moonrise.
Our module skims the bleak surface –
A torchlight beam. We've orbited twice,

We are as near to landing as men
Can be in absolute zero.
Ice whorled and twisted. Ice as smooth
As mile-wide mirrors. Ice, and again
More ice. Walls. Mountains. Sculpted snow.
Giants' fingers caught in the groove

Of ice-maids' breasts. We draw on myth
To describe the terror of this last
Beyond of the beyonds. I brought
Dante to read. His hell ends with
The absolute ice, the cosmic blast
Of winds from Satan's wings. Here thought

Freezes – let alone bodies. That moon:
They named it Charon – ferryman
To Pluto's underworld. But we're

Not in Hades… Only… we'll soon
Freeze into sleep, sleep into an
Unknown… and will we wake? Ice. Fear.

This planet – which looks even worse
Than Satan's hole where Dante's fixed him
Chewing Judas for eternity –
Is no hell, no. Here we, the first
Humans to leave our solar system,
Gaze our last at our own country,

Land's End… receding… We're for deep space –
Black void of cryogenic sleep.
Soon we'll be only a fading blip
On NASA computer screens. A guess –
Backed up by simulations, a leap
From mathematical models – flip

Of a coin, more like – has plotted a course
To one planet orbiting one star
They calculate – gamble – has life.
And we – of the Interstellar Force –
Have gambled our lives, lifetimes… for
If we make it back earthwards, if

We walk through Earth's bluebells again
It'll be two centuries later, and we
Will fumble like Neanderthals
Up indecipherable hitech men,
Trusting they'll bother to read CVs
On flawed computer-disks… Our souls

Floating between two unrelated
Periods of history… like Drake's
Golden Hind crew dumped on the moon

To meet Neil Armstrong by his crater
In nineteen sixty-nine. We'd ache
From asking questions, we'd be baboons

In lab experiments… I guess
None of us reckon we'll make it back.
What will we see… if we wake up?
Now I see only Earth's loveliness:
An opening rose, the thump and thwack
Of my dog's tail, beechwoods that slope

Up the chalk downs to an ancient camp
Where frightened Celts fought off the Saxons…
Our rockets fire. A last dim glimpse
Of Charon's ice – hell's river. The lamp
Of our sun fades… fades… Deep space blacks us
Out from thought, drags us over the rim

Of the known universe, into
The beyond's private unconsciousness.
A few more hours. Pluto recedes.
That absolute ice is our last view
Of not Earth, but Earth… I signed 'Yes',
Consented… Now. Lie down. Drip feeds

Fixed. The injection. Last man does
Himself. Cool, cool, but like a blanket
Wrapping me up. The motor buzz –
A bee-sting, so gentle… I think it…

R.S. THOMAS

The New Mariner

In the silence
that is his chosen medium
of communication and telling
others about it
in words. Is there no way
not to be the sport
of reason? For me now
there is only the God-space
into which I send out
my probes. I had looked forward
to old age as a time
of quietness, a time to draw
my horizons about me,
to watch memories ripening
in the sunlight of a walled garden.
But there is the void
over my head and the distance
within that the tireless signals
come from. And astronaut
on impossible journeys
to the far side of the self
I return with messages
I cannot decipher, garrulous
about them, worrying the ear
of the passer-by, hot on his way
to the marriage of plain fact with plain fact.

LAVINIA GREENLAW

For the First Dog in Space

You're being sent up in Sputnik 2,
a kind of octopus with rigor mortis.
Ground control have sworn allegiance
to gravity and the laws of motion;
they sleep without dreams,
safe in the knowledge
that a Russian mongrel bitch
can be blasted through the exosphere
at seven miles a second,
but can never stray far from home.
You will have no companion,
no buttons to press, just six days' air.
Laika, do not let yourself be fooled
by the absolute stillness
that comes with now knowing
how fast you are going. As you fall
in orbit around the earth, remember
your language. Listen to star dust.
Trust your fear.

TOM SLEIGH

For a Spacesuit Set Adrift

*NASA had reported that the 'SuitSat' device [a Russian spacesuit
equipped with a radio transmitter and stuffed with old clothes that
was set adrift from the International Space Station] had ceased
working within hours of its release on Friday. But a US amateur
radio spokesman said weak signals had been picked up. 'Death
reports were premature,' he said.*

BBC

1

Under the starflood where
the flood of earth confronts her,
tiny, unmoored, drifting upside down,
the ocean's pupil peers into her helmet's faceplate:

voices hiss and crackle... *too late... your fault...*
It's not what she did but what
she did not do that haunts her.

Ears ache with intonations calling
from dimensions beyond the three she knows
where the dead come and go,
where absurd consolations talk inside her helmet.

Who gave the order that made her take this walk
past the corner comet, the next door asteroid?
Why, why was she shoved out into this void?

2

Think of mayhem out in space, matter-hungry black holes
that flay their stellar neighbors, fields of gravitation
that crush matter to nearly nothing, galaxies
colliding and eating one another –
all of it going on in invisible bands of the spectrum
nobody at a funeral is aware of in the music,
in the way the mourner leans over the coffin and strokes the wood.

Marooned where nobody can reach her,
her abandonment expanding like the decimals of *pi*,
she senses the dead approaching, here, here –
the dead that the ones down there

glued to their antennae so desire and fear.
They shove her out the airlock, they shove her out again,
again the void fills her suit the way it fills the dark she floats in.

3

No way through, no way out but this:
or so say the ones that track her
while earth crackles with a plea
please please don't ever leave me

But voices of the dead decay
into babble of the radio bubble
spreading ever wider and deeper into space.

The split second delay between when their mouths open
and the sound reaches her ear
takes the measure of her already changed position
as if all she needs to do is step out into the tenth dimension

where her old dresses and blouses come to life once more –
but space curls and curves away…
How she loathes infinity. She moves where the void moves her.

4

She dreams of the mothership.
She dreams of gravity.
She dreams space as her unbrokenness,
her body touching everywhere.

She's back before the big bang,
before anyone can laugh at her,
before her body can abandon her

and love drifts away.
She forgets past and future,
she doesn't grow older or younger,
no tears distort her eyes.

Her ears are closed to everything.
Every signal is decayed.
All space compresses into her smile.

EDWIN MORGAN

The First Men on Mercury

– We come in peace from the third planet.
Would you take us to your leader?

– Bawr stretter! Bawr. Bawr. Stretterhawl?

– This is a little plastic model
of the solar system, with working parts.
You are here and we are there and we
are now here with you, is that clear?

– Gawl horrop. Bawr. Abawrhannahanna!

– Where we come from is blue and white
with brown, you see we call the brown
here 'land', the blue is 'sea', and the white
is 'clouds' over land and sea, we live
on the surface of the brown land,
all round is sea and clouds. We are 'men'.
Men come –

– Glawp men! Gawrbenner menko. Menhawl?

– Men come in peace from the third planet
which we call 'earth'. We are earthmen.
Take us earthmen to your leader.

– Thmen? Thmen? Bawr. Bawrhossop.
Yuleeda tan hanna. Harrabost yuleeda.

– I am the yuleeda. You see my hands,
we carry no benner, we come in peace.
The spaceways are all stretterhawn.

– Glawn peacemen all horrabhanna tantko!
Tan come at'mstrossop. Glawp yuleeda!

– Atoms are peacegawl in our harraban.
Menbat worrabost from tan hannahanna.

– You men we know bawrhossoptant. Bawr.
We know yuleeda. Go strawg backspetter quick.

– We cantantabawr, tantingko backspetter now!

– Banghapper now! Yes, third planet back.
Yuleeda will go back blue, white, brown
nowhanna! There is no more talk.

– Gawl han fasthapper?

– No. You must go back to your planet.
Go back in peace, take what you have gained
but quickly.

– Stretterworra gawl, gawl…

– Of course, but nothing is ever the same,
now is it? You'll remember Mercury.

CRAIG RAINE

A Martian Sends a Postcard Home

Caxtons are mechanical birds with many wings
and some are treasured for their markings –

they cause the eyes to melt
or the body to shriek without pain.

I have never seen one fly, but
sometimes they perch on the hand.

Mist is when the sky is tired of flight
and rests its soft machine on ground:

then the world is dim and bookish
like engravings under tissue paper.

Rain is when the earth is television.
It has the property of making colours darker.

Model T is a room with the lock inside –
a key is turned to free the world

for movement, so quick there is a film
to watch for anything missed.

But time is tied to the wrist
or kept in a box, ticking with impatience.

In homes, a haunted apparatus sleeps,
that snores when you pick it up.

If the ghost cries, they carry it
to their lips and soothe it to sleep

with sounds. And yet, they wake it up
deliberately, by tickling it with a finger.

Only the young are allowed to suffer
openly. Adults go to a punishment room

with water but nothing to eat.
They lock the door and suffer the noises

alone. No one is exempt
and everyone's pain has a different smell.

At night, when all the colours die,
they hide in pairs

and read about themselves –
in colour, with their eyelids shut.

BILLY COLLINS

Earthling

You have probably come across
those scales in planetariums
that tell you how much you
would weigh on other planets.

You have noticed the fat ones
lingering on the Mars scale
and the emaciated slowing up
the line for Neptune.

As a creature of average weight,
I fail to see the attraction.

Imagine squatting in the wasteland
of Pluto, all five tons of you,
or wandering around Mercury
wondering what to do next with your ounce.

How much better to step onto
the simple bathroom scale,
a happy earthling feeling
the familiar ropes of gravity,

157 pounds standing soaking wet
a respectful distance from the sun.

GREG DELANTY

The Alien

I'm back again scutinising the Milky Way
    of your ultrasound, scanning the dark
      matter, the nothingness, that now the heads say
    is chockablock with quarks & squarks,
gravitons & gravitini, photons & photinos. Our sprout,

who art there inside the spacecraft
    of your Ma, the time capsule of this printout,
      hurling & whirling towards us, it's all daft
    on this earth. Our alien who art in the heavens,
our Martian, our little green man, we're anxious

to make contact, to ask divers questions
    about the heavendom you hail from, to discuss
      the whole shebang of the beginning&end,
    the pre-big bang untime before you forget the why
and lie of thy first place. And, our friend,

to say Welcome, that we mean no harm, we'd die
    for you even, that we pray you're not here
      to subdue us, that we'd put away
    our ray guns, missiles, attitude and share
our world with you, little big head, if only you stay.

JAMIE McKENDRICK

Out There

If space begins at an indefinite zone
where the chance of two gas molecules colliding
is rarer than a green dog or a blue moon
then that's as near as we can get to nothing.

Nostalgia for the earth and its atmosphere
weakens the flesh and bones of cosmonauts.
One woke to find his crewmate in a space suit
and asked where he was going. For a walk.

He had to sleep between him and the air-lock.
Another heard a dog bark and a child cry
halfway to the moon. What once had been

where heaven was, is barren beyond imagining,
and never so keenly as from out there can
the lost feel earth's the only paradise.

ROBERT FROST

Desert Places

Snow falling and night falling fast, oh, fast
In a field I looked into going past,
And the ground almost covered smooth in snow,
But a few weeds and stubble showing last.

The woods around it have it – it is theirs.
All animals are smothered in their lairs.
I am too absent-spirited to count;
The loneliness includes me unawares.

And lonely as it is, that loneliness
Will be more lonely ere it will be less –
A blanker whiteness of benighted snow
With no expression, nothing to express.

They cannot scare me with their empty spaces
Between stars – on stars where no human race is.
I have it in me so much nearer home
To scare myself with my own desert places.

NICK LAIRD

The Effects

for Paul Murdin

To see the gods withdraw,
dethroned, exposed to ridicule,
was our allotted truth –
and not without its suffering.

They weren't dislodged
by other, stronger gods;
they simply came to nothing.
That line of enquiry closed.

*

Stars, too, are born and die.
One might collapse in space-time.
Be massive; compact; vanish.
Amid photographs of supernovae,

the neon pulsing plasma cauls,
is this rudimentary study done
with a compass and a pencil;
Black hole (artist's impression).

In modern death, no light escapes.
Time stops. You cannot see it, only
note the wobble of the bodies
on their axes, in their orbits.

*

And your *Catalogue of the Universe*
has Cookstown District Cemetery,
hundreds sternly packed graveside
and then, mid-hymn, a dog gets free.

The animal you cannot see, only
how the faces turn, one-by-one
and radiant, to watch the mongrel
pass so desperately among them.

WILLIAM EMPSON

Letter I

You were amused to find you too could fear
'The eternal silence of the infinite spaces',
That net-work without fish, that mere
Extended idleness, those pointless places
Who, being possibilized to bear faces,
Yours and the light from it, up-buoyed,
Even of the galaxies are void.

I approve, myself, dark spaces between stars;
All privacy's their gift; they carry glances
Through gulfs; and as for messages (thus Mars'
Renown for wisdom their wise tact enhances,
Hanged on the thread of radio advances)
For messages, they are a wise go-between,
And say what they think common-sense has seen.

Only, have we space, common-sense in common,
A tribe whose life-blood is our sacrament,
Physics or metaphysics for your showman,
For my physician in this banishment?
Too non-Euclidean predicament.
Where is that darkness that gives light its place?
Or where such darkness as would hide your face?

Our jovial sun, if he avoids exploding
(These times are critical), will cease to grin,
Will lose your circumambient foreboding;
Loose the full radiance his mass can win
While packed with mass holds all that radiance in;
Flame far too hot not to seem utter cold
And hide a tumult never to be told.

EDWARD THOMAS

Out in the Dark

Out in the dark over the snow
The fallow fawns invisible go
With the fallow doe;
And the winds blow
Fast as the stars are slow.

Stealthily the dark haunts round
And, when a lamp goes, without sound
At a swifter bound
Than the swiftest hound,
Arrives, and all else is drowned;

And I and star and wind and deer
Are in the dark together, – near,
Yet far, – and fear
Drums on my ear
In that sage company drear.

How weak and little is the light,
All the universe of sight,
Love and delight,
Before the might,
If you love it not, of night.

GEORGE GORDON, LORD BYRON

Darkness

I had a dream, which was not all a dream.
The bright sun was extinguish'd, and the stars
Did wander darkling in the eternal space,
Rayless, and pathless, and the icy earth
Swung blind and blackening in the moonless air;
Morn came and went – and came, and brought no day,
And men forgot their passions in the dread
Of this their desolation; and all hearts
Were chill'd into a selfish prayer for light:
And they did live by watchfires – and the thrones,
The palaces of crowned kings – the huts,
The habitations of all things which dwell,
Were burnt for beacons; cities were consumed,
And men were gather'd round their blazing homes
To look once more into each other's face;
Happy were those who dwelt within the eye
Of the volcanos, and their mountain-torch:
A fearful hope was all the world contain'd;
Forests were set on fire – but hour by hour
They fell and faded – and the crackling trunks
Extinguish'd with a crash – and all was black.
The brows of men by the despairing light
Wore an unearthly aspect, as by fits
The flashes fell upon them; some lay down
And hid their eyes and wept; and some did rest
Their chins upon their clenched hands, and smiled;
And others hurried to and fro, and fed
Their funeral piles with fuel, and look'd up
With mad disquietude on the dull sky,
The pall of a past world; and then again

With curses cast them down upon the dust,
And gnash'd their teeth and howl'd: the wild birds shriek'd,
And, terrified, did flutter on the ground,
And flap their useless wings; the wildest brutes
Came tame and tremulous; and vipers crawl'd
And twined themselves among the multitude,
Hissing, but stingless – they were slain for food:
And War, which for a moment was no more,
Did glut himself again; – a meal was bought
With blood, and each sate sullenly apart
Gorging himself in gloom: no love was left;
All earth was but one thought – and that was death,
Immediate and inglorious; and the pang
Of famine fed upon all entrails – men
Died, and their bones were tombless as their flesh;
The meagre by the meagre were devour'd,
Even dogs assail'd their masters, all save one,
And he was faithful to a corse, and kept
The birds and beasts and famish'd men at bay,
Till hunger clung them, or the dropping dead
Lured their lank jaws; himself sought out no food,
But with a piteous and perpetual moan,
And a quick desolate cry, licking the hand
Which answer'd not with a caress – he died.
The crowd was famish'd by degrees; but two
Of an enormous city did survive,
And they were enemies: they met beside
The dying embers of an altar-place
Where had been heap'd a mass of holy things
For an unholy usage; they raked up,
And shivering scraped with their cold skeleton hands
The feeble ashes, and their feeble breath
Blew for a little life, and made a flame
Which was a mockery; then they lifted up
Their eyes as it grew lighter, and beheld

Each other's aspects – saw, and shriek'd, and died –
Even of their mutual hideousness they died,
Unknowing who he was upon whose brow
Famine had written Fiend. The world was void,
The populous and the powerful was a lump,
Seasonless, herbless, treeless, manless, lifeless –
A lump of death – a chaos of hard clay.
The rivers, lakes and ocean all stood still,
And nothing stirr'd within their silent depths;
Ships sailorless lay rotting on the sea,
And their masts fell down piecemeal: as they dropp'd
They slept on the abyss without a surge –
The waves were dead; the tides were in their grave,
The Moon, their mistress, had expir'd before;
The winds were wither'd in the stagnant air,
And the clouds perish'd; Darkness had no need
Of aid from them – She was the Universe.

REBECCA ELSON

Let There Always Be Light
(Searching for Dark Matter)

For this we go out dark nights, searching
For the dimmest stars,
For signs of unseen things:

To weigh us down.
To stop the universe
From rushing on and on
Into its own beyond
Till it exhausts itself and lies down cold,
Its last star going out.

Whatever they turn out to be,
Let there be swarms of them,
Enough for immortality,
Always a star where we can warm ourselves.

Let there be enough to bring it back
From its own edges,
To bring us all so close that we ignite
The bright spark of resurrection.

Ode to Heaven

Chorus of Spirits

FIRST SPIRIT:
Palace-roof of cloudless nights!
Paradise of golden lights!
   Deep, immeasurable, vast,
Which art now, and which wert then
   Of the Present and the Past,
Of the eternal Where and When,
   Presence-chamber, temple, home,
   Ever-canopying dome,
   Of acts and ages yet to come!

Glorious shapes have life in thee,
Earth, and all earth's company;
   Living globes which ever throng
Thy deep chasms and wildernesses;
   And green worlds that glide along;
And swift stars with flashing tresses;
   And icy moons most cold and bright,
   And mighty suns beyond the night,
   Atoms of intensest light.

Even thy name is as a god,
Heaven! for thou art the abode
   Of that Power which is the glass
Wherein man his nature sees.
   Generations as they pass
Worship thee with bended knees.
   Their unremaining gods and they

Like a river roll away:
Thou remainest such – alway! –

SECOND SPIRIT:
Thou art but the mind's first chamber,
Round which its young fancies clamber,
    Like weak insects in a cave,
Lighted up by stalactites;
    But the portal of the grave
Where a world of new delights
    Will make thy best glories seem
    But a dim and noonday gleam
    From the shadow of a dream!

THIRD SPIRIT:
Peace! the abyss is wreathed with scorn
At your presumption, atom-born!
    What is Heaven? and what are ye
Who its brief expanse inherit?
    What are suns and spheres which flee
With the instinct of that Spirit
    Of which ye are but a part?
    Drops which Nature's mighty heart
    Drives through thinnest veins! Depart!

What is Heaven? a globe of dew,
Filling in the morning new
    Some eyed flower whose young leaves waken
On an unimagined world:
    Constellated suns unshaken,
Orbits measureless, are furled
    In that frail and fading sphere,
    With ten millions gathered there,
    To tremble, gleam, and disappear.

WILLIAM SHAKESPEARE

from The Merchant of Venice

V, i, 54–65

LORENZO:

How sweet the moonlight sleeps upon this bank!
Here will we sit, and let the sounds of music
Creep in our ears – soft stillness and the night
Become the touches of sweet harmony:
Sit, Jessica, – look, how the floor of heaven
Is thick inlaid with patens of bright gold,
There's not the smallest orb which thou behold'st
But in his motion like an angel sings,
Still quiring to the young-ey'd cherubins;
Such harmony is in immortal souls,
But whilst this muddy vesture of decay
Doth grossly close it in, we cannot hear it.

JOHN DONNE

from Of the Progress of the Soul

[The soul's liberty by death]

But think that death hath now enfranchised thee,
Thou hast thy expansion now, and liberty;
Think that a rusty piece, discharged, is flown
In pieces, and the bullet is his own,
And freely flies; this to thy soul allow,
Think thy shell broke, think thy soul hatched but now.
And think this slow-paced soul, which late did cleave
To a body, and went but by the body's leave,
Twenty, perchance, or thirty mile a day,
Dispatches in a minute all the way
'Twixt heaven, and earth: she stays not in the air,
To look what meteors there themselves prepare;
She carries no desire to know, nor sense,
Whether th' air's middle region be intense;
For th' element of fire, she doth not know,
Whether she passed by such a place or no;
She baits not at the moon, nor cares to try
Whether in that new world, men live and die.
Venus retards her not, to inquire, how she
Can, (being one star) Hesper, and Vesper be;
He that charmed Argus' eyes, sweet Mercury,
Works not on her, who now is grown all eye;
Who, if she meets the body of the sun,
Goes through, not staying till his course be run;
Who finds in Mars his camp, no corps of guard;
Nor is by Jove, nor by his father barred;
But ere she can consider how she went,
At once is at, and through the firmament.

GREG DELANTY

The Event Horizon

Perhaps, those zones where our souls are said to end up
        are possible: that region the good inhabit,
the zone the imperfect are burnished perfect, the infernal place
        of no hopers. The afterlife is no more unbelievable
than us landed here on this giant spinning-top
        speeding crookedly through the cosmos,

especially now the spacebrains proclaim zones
        where time's altered, kaput; dimensions where stars slip
through self-generated cracks in space and so much more
        not dreamed of in our reality. Truly, after all,
the soul has somewhere to go beyond the only event horizon
        we know, our point of no return. How unbelievable.

THOM GUNN

My Sad Captains

One by one they appear in
the darkness: a few friends, and
a few with historical
names. How late they start to shine!
but before they fade they stand
perfectly embodied, all

the past lapping them like a
cloak of chaos. They were men
who, I thought, lived only to
renew the wasteful force they
spent with each hot convulsion.
They remind me, distant now.

True, they are not at rest yet,
but now that they are indeed
apart, winnowed from failures,
they withdraw to an orbit
and turn with disinterested
hard energy, like the stars.

HENRY VAUGHAN

'They are All Gone into the World of Light!'

They are all gone into the world of light!
    And I alone sit ling'ring here;
Their very memory is fair and bright,
       And my sad thoughts doth clear.

It glows and glitters in my cloudy breast
    Like stars upon some gloomy grove,
Or those faint beams in which this hill is dressed,
       After the sun's remove.

I see them walking in an air of glory,
    Whose light doth trample on my days:
My days, which are at best but dull and hoary,
       Mere glimmering and decays.

O holy hope! And high humility,
    High as the Heavens above!
These are your walks, and you have showed them me
       To kindle my cold love,

Dear, beauteous death! the jewel of the just,
    Shining nowhere, but in the dark;
What mysteries do lie beyond thy dust;
       Could man outlook that mark!

He that hath found some fledged bird's nest, may know
    At first sight, if the bird be flown;
But what fair well, or grove he sings in now,
       That is to him unknown.

And yet, as Angels in some brighter dreams
    Call to the soul, when man doth sleep:
So some strange thoughts transcend our wonted themes,
      And into glory peep.

If a star were confined into a tomb
    Her captive flames must needs burn there;
But when the hand that locked her up, gives room,
      She'll shine through all the sphere.

O Father of eternal life, and all
    Created glories under thee!
Resume thy spirit from this world of thrall
      Into true liberty.

Either disperse these mists, which blot and fill
    My perspective (still) as they pass;
Or else remove me hence unto that hill,
      Where I shall need no glass.

DERYN REES-JONES

A Dream of Constellations

.-- ..... . -./ - ..... ./ -- --- -. - ....-/ - ..... .- -/ .-- .-. ./ .-.. ..... - / -.-. ---
..- .-. .-. -..-/ - ..... / ..... .-.. -../ .. -./ --- ..- .-./ ..... .- -. -.. ... /

.. / .-- .-. -. - . -..-/ - --- / .... .-. .- .- -.-- .--/ - ..... - / .. / -.-. --- ..- .-. -.. /
-. -- --- .-.-.- / - ..... ./ .- .... - .- .- -. -.-. -. - .- .-. ../ -.-. .-. -.. -.. /

- ..... .- -/ ..-. --- .-. .- - .-../ .- -. -.. ./ --. .-. .-. - / .. -. ...... -.. / .-. -- --- ..-
.-. ./ -..... .-. .- -. -. ./

..-. --- .-. .-. --- .- .. -. --/ ..... .- .-. ./ .-. .. .- -. . .--/ .... .-. . . . -.--/ ..... .-. . -.
..... / .-. .. .- -. .... --.--/ -..... -. .-. -. . -. -. -. ../ .. -. --.-- /

-..... .-. .. .. -. --. .. -. . -. ./ -.-- --- ..-/ .... --- -. -. --.--/ -.. .. ..-.. .-
.-. -. - . -. --./ -.-- --- ..- .-. .-./ .... .-. .-. . . -. --.-- /

-..... .-. .-- --- ..- --- ..... - / .. .-- ..../ .- - / -.. .. --. ....- / - ..... .- -/ .-- .- ...
..... -.. -. . .-. -.- .-.-.- / -.-. -. --- .-. -. -. ... --.-- /

-..... .- - / -. .--- --- / .- .... ../ .. - ... .-. .-. .-. .-. -.-.-/ .- -. -.. / .... --- --.-- / .-. .. ..
-.- ./ .- - / - ....-. .. .- -- / .- --- / - --- / -..../ .... .-. ..- --- .-. -.-. -.--.- /

....-. -.. . . -. -.-. ./ - ..... .- -. .- .- -..-/ .. - .- -. .-. -. -.. ../ .. - -. . - /
- ..../ - -. . .--/ .-. -. -.. .- ..... --.-- /

- ..... ./ -. .. .- .-- -. .- -. - .-.. -. -. -.../ .-. - -. -.. / --- -- -. . ./ --- -- -. .-. ./
. .-.. ... ... -. . --.-- /

- ..... .- .. ./ -. . . .-. .-. -.- - -. -.. ../ .- .- -. -.. / ... -. - . -. . . .-. .-. -. -. ../ --- -- ...-. /
- .- .. . ./ .-- --- --- -. .-. -. -.. .-. -. --.-- /

- .. .-- --./ ..... .-. . -.-. ../ .- -. -. -.. / ..... .-. .- -- --- .-. -. -.. .-.-./ - ..... ./ -.-. --- -. -. ...
- -. .-. - . -. .- -.-- --- -. --- -. .-. / ..... .-- .- .... -. -..-/

-..... .-. .. -. . -. -. -. -. .-. ../ .- -. - / --- .-- -. .- -. -. -. .-. -. - .-. ./ .. .. -./ .-. -. -. -. .- .- -. .-.
. ...../ --- --.-./ -.. .. . .. -. .- / .- -.-. -. -. -. /

- --- --.-.-. .- ..... .-./ .== ./ .-.. .-.. === === · . . ./ .. · · ·/ ---- / - ..... ./
... -.- -.-. /

.- ..-/ ..- .-. .-. ..... -/ -- .. -. --- .-. ./ -..... .-.-. -. -- . -- ../ - ..... / ..... .- .-. -. .- ..- .-. -. . ... /
-..... .- .. -. .-. --.-- /

- ..... / - .- .- .- ..-././ .... --- --- -. .../ --- .-. -.../ -.-. .-. -. - --- ... -.-. / .- .-. -. -. ../ .-. -. ---
.-. .- .- -.-. .- -.-. --.-- / .- ..- -. .. -.-. -.-. -. -.-. ... .-. -. --.-- / .- .- -. .. ..-. -. .. -..
--.-- /

For a text version of the poem, see page 230.

GERARD MANLEY HOPKINS

Spelt from Sibyl's Leaves

Earnest, earthless, equal, attuneable, ǀ vaulty, voluminous, …
stupendous
Evening strains to be tíme's vást, ǀ womb-of-all, home-of-all,
hearse-of-all night.
Her fond yellow hornlight wound to the west, ǀ her wild hollow
hoarlight hung to the height
Waste; her earliest stars, earlstars, ǀ stárs principal, overbend us,
Fíre-féaturing heaven. For earth ǀ her being has unbound; her
dapple is at end, as-
Tray or aswarm, all throughther, in throngs; ǀ self ín self steepèd
and páshed – qúite
Disremembering, dísmémbering ǀ áll now. Heart, you round me
right
With: Óur évening is over us; óur night ǀ whélms, whélms, ánd
will end us.
Only the beakleaved boughs dragonish ǀ damask the tool-smooth
bleak light; black,
Ever so black on it. Óur tale, O óur oracle! ǀ Lét life, wáned, ah lét life
wind
Off hér once skéined stained véined varíety ǀ upon, áll on twó
spools; párt, pen, páck
Now her áll in twó flocks, twó folds – black, white; ǀ right, wrong;
reckon but, reck but, mind
But thése two: wáre of a wórld where bút these ǀ twó tell, each off the
óther; of a rack
Where, selfwrung, selfstrung, sheathe- and shelterless, ǀ thóughts
agaínst thoughts ín groans grínd.

LES MURRAY

Infra Red

for Prof. Fred Hoyle and the IRAS telescope

Dark stars that never fire,
brown dwarfs, whose deepening collapse
inward on themselves never tightens to fuse glory,
scorched dust the size of worlds, and tenuous
sandbags strung between the galaxies,
a universe dull with life:

with the eye and eye-adjuncts
mind sees only what is burning, the peak nodes of fury
that make all spiralling in on them
or coronally near, blowing outward from them,
look eager, intense, even brave. Most of the real
however is obscurely reflective, just sauntering along,
yarning across a ditch, or watching television,
vaguely dreaming, perhaps about pubic stuff,

getting tea ready. This absorbs most of the light
but is also family. It impoverishes to unreality
not to consider the dim, cannon fodder of stardom,
the gravities they are steepening to,
the unfathomable from which the trite is spoken.
And starry science is an evening paper astrology
without the unknown bodies registered
only by total pain, only by dazzled joy,
the transits marked by a tight grip of the heart.

That the visible stars are suburbs and slow towns
hyped to light speed is the testimony of debris
and the serious swarms at rest in migrant trajectories.

Brilliance stands accused of all their losses.
Presence perhaps, and the interference of presence,
not light, should found a more complete astronomy.

It will draw in absence, too:
the pain-years between a love and its fulfilment,
the intricate spiral space of suppressed tradition
and all the warmth, whose peaks aren't those of heat,
that the white dwarfs froze out of their galaxies.

JOHN DONNE

from An Anatomy of the World

[*Disformity of Parts*]

We think the heavens enjoy their spherical,
Their round proportion embracing all.
But yet their various and perplexed course,
Observed in divers ages, doth enforce
Men to find out so many eccentric parts,
Such divers down-right lines, such overthwarts,
As disproportion that pure form. It tears
The firmament in eight and forty shares,
And in these constellations then arise
New stars, and old do vanish from our eyes:
As though heaven suffered earthquakes, peace or war,
When new towers rise, and old demolished are.
They have impaled within a zodiac
The free-born sun, and keep twelve signs awake
To watch his steps; the goat and crab control,
And fright him back, who else to either pole
(Did not these tropics fetter him) might run:
For his course is not round; nor can the sun
Perfect a circle, or maintain his way
One inch direct; but where he rose today
He comes no more, but with a cozening line,
Steals by that point, and so is serpentine:
And seeming weary with his reeling thus,
He means to sleep, being now fall'n nearer us.
So, of the stars which boast that they do run
In circle still, none ends where he begun.
All their proportion's lame, it sinks, it swells.

For of meridians, and parallels,
Man hath weaved out a net, and this net thrown
Upon the heavens, and now they are his own.

HENRY VAUGHAN

The Sphere of Archimedes out of Claudian

When Jove a heaven of small glass did behold,
He smiled, and to the gods these words he told.
Comes then the power of man's art to this?
In a frail orb my work new acted is.
The poles' decrees, the fate of things: God's laws
Down by his art old Archimedes draws.
Spirits enclosed the several stars attend,
And orderly the living work they bend.
A feignèd Zodiac measures out the year,
Every new month a false Moon doth appear.
And now bold industry is proud, it can
Wheel round its world, and rule the stars by man.
Why at Salmoneus' thunder do I stand?
Nature is rivalled by a single hand.

PAUL MULDOON

Ontario

I spent last night in the nursery of a house in Pennsylvania. When I put out the light I made my way, barefoot, through the aftermath of Brandywine Creek. The constellations of the northern hemisphere were picked out in luminous paint on the ceiling. I lay under a comforting, phosphorescent Plough, thinking about where the Plough stopped being the Plough and became the Big Dipper. About the astronomer I met in Philadelphia who had found a star with a radio telescope. The star is now named after her, whatever her name happens to be. As all these stars grew dim, it seemed like a good time to rerun my own dream-visions. They had flashed up just as I got into bed on three successive nights in 1972. The first was a close-up of a face, Cox's face, falling. I heard next morning how he had come home drunk and taken a nose-dive down the stairs. Next, my uncle Pat's face, falling in slo-mo like the first, but bloody. It turned out he had slipped off a ladder on a building-site. His forehead needed seven stitches. Lastly, a freeze-frame trickle of water or glycerine on a sheet of smoked glass or perspex. I see it in shaving-mirrors. Dry Martinis. Women's tears. On windshields. As planes take off or land. I remembered how I was meant to fly to Toronto this morning, to visit my younger brother. He used to be a research assistant at the University of Guelph, where he wrote a thesis on nitrogen-fixing in soya beans, or symbiosis, or some such mystery. He now works for the Corn Producers' Association of Ontario. On my last trip we went to a disco in the Park Plaza, where I helped a girl in a bin-liner dress to find her contact-lens.

– Did you know that Spinoza was a lens-grinder?

– Are you for real?

Joe was somewhere in the background, sniggering, flicking cosmic dandruff from his shoulders.

– A lens, I went on, is really a lentil. A pulse.

Her back was an imponderable, green furrow in the ultra-violet strobe.

– Did *you* know that Yonge Street's the longest street in the world?
– I can't say that I did.
– Well, it starts a thousand miles to the north, and it ends right here.

FREDERICK SEIDEL

from The Cosmos Trilogy

12 Invisible Dark Matter

It is the invisible
Dark matter we are not made of
That I am afraid of.
Most of the universe consists of this.

I put a single normal ice cube
In my drink.
It weighs one hundred million tons.
It is a sample from the densest star.

I read my way across
The awe I wrote
That you are reading now.
I can't believe that you are there

Except you are. I wonder what
Cosmologists don't know
That could be everything
There is.

The someone looking at the page
Could be the everything there is,
Material that shines,
Or shined.

Dark matter is another
Matter. Cosmologists don't know.

The physicists do not.
The stars are not.

Another thing beside
The row of things is
Standing there. It is invisible,
And reads without a sound.

It doesn't matter
That it doesn't really.
I need to take its hand
To cross the street.

18 Supersymmetry

You step into the elevator
To go down and it goes up,
And the surprise
Of the sensation of sudden

Happiness is weightless.
So is love.
The chemistry of intergalactic
Space is scarcely human,

But on the other hand we
Are all related.
So is love.
Einstein bicycled right here, didn't he?

The guru Edward Witten, talking
Along the same Princeton streets many years after
And into the grounds of the Institute
For Advanced Study, is not lost.

He zooms to a blackboard
Of equations about
The quantum mechanics
Of the central thing when it is raining outside.

He titters behind
The flutter of a geisha fan,
In heavy makeup, left, right, male, female,
Kabuki, kooky.

Over the ocean in France, the platinum meter stick
Under a glass bell is rational,

And meaningless,
And dissolving.

But Witten grasps it cheerily in one hand
And the geisha fan in the other,
Like the pots of gold at the ends of the rainbow
In the rain.

25 The Birth of the Universe

The perfect petals
Of the rose
Of time, of all three
Angels that prepare for this,

Of everything the blue
Warm water does
To magnify the August hour,
The perfect

Thunder mint
Between the thumb and finger
Makes, or the large smell of rain before it rains,
Grow from several storm cells

Violently,
While the hour
Hand sweeps as if it were barking seconds
And the day stands still,

In perfect bloom,
And so the universe,
Was just conceived,
And just arrives,

And jets a rising fountain
Lit with many lights
And colors,
And a rushing sound,

And it is night,
And it is air,

And the ice cream is infinite
Above the cone

The small hand holds
Dripping, holds the torch
Of everything
Is good.

37 Star Bright

The story goes one day
A messenger from light arrived.
Of course they never know that they're a messenger.
Don't know they carry a message.

The submarine stayed just
Below the surface with its engines off near the shore observing.
One day the world took off its shoes and disappeared
Inside the central mosque

And never came back out. Outside the periscope the rain
Had stopped, the fires on shore were
Out. Outside the mosque
The vast empty plaza was the city's outdoor market till

The satellite observed the changing
Colors of the planet
And reported to the submarine that
No one was alive.

A messenger from light arrived.
Of course they never know that they're a messenger.
Don't know they carry a message.
And then they stay a while and then they leave.

Arrived, was ushered in,
Got in a waiting car and drove away.
Was ushered in,
Kowtowed to the Sacred Presence the required ten times

And backed away from the Sacred Presence blind,
And turned back into light.

Good night,
Blind light.

Far star, star bright.
And though they never know that they're a messenger,
Never know they carry a message,
At least they stay a while before they leave.

GEORGE BRADLEY

About Planck Time

Once upon a time, way back in the infinitesimal
First fraction of a second attending our creation,
A tiny drop containing all of it, all energy
And all its guises, burst upon the scene,
Exploding out of nothing into everything
Virtually instantaneously, the way our thoughts
Leap eagerly to occupy the abhorrent void.
Once, say ten or twenty billion years ago,
In Planck time, in no time at all, the veil
Available to our perceptions was flung out
Over space at such a rate the mere imagination
Cannot keep up, so rapidly the speed of light
Lags miraculously behind, producing a series
Of incongruities that has led our curiosity,
Like Ariadne's thread, through the dim labyrinth
Of our conclusions to the place of our beginning.
In Planck time, everything that is was spread so thin
That all distance is enormous, between each star,
Between subatomic particles, so that we are composed
Almost entirely of emptiness, so that what separates
This world, bright ball floating in its midnight blue,
From the irrefutable logic of no world at all
Has no more substance than the traveler's dream,
So that nothing can be said for certain except
That sometime, call it Planck time, it will all just
Disappear, a parlor trick, a rabbit back in its hat,
Will all go up in a flash of light, abracadabra,
An idea that isn't being had anymore.

KATHRYN MARIS

Why

Before I was God
as you know Him to be
I liked to sit
on my quark bench
and stretch my legs,
take in the void,
have a snooze
then wake and sketch
plans for the future.

There was no time
and then there was –
too much time –
and as I have eyes
on the back of my head
I saw it all:
the beginning, the end,
and all the carnage
in between.

When I sat on the bench
I used to like
looking at
a pagoda I made
from the finest wood
from the first tree
that would make no sound
when it hit the earth
in an earless time.

And then one day
I was disturbed
by a sound
that was a word
like 'I' or 'sky'
(it wasn't clear)
and I looked to find
there was a man
in my pagoda!

I could only conclude
his word was 'why':
he repeated himself
and had no legs
and probably was
sorry for himself,
but it was hard to hear
and harder to see
from my preferred distance.

I saw him better
with binoculars,
but had forgotten his name
and the era of his suffering
and where he was from –
then or now –
though it's all the same,
and they all say 'why' –
it's the Question of the Day.

I know I could have
banished him
but I let him stay
for he gave me ideas
and though I didn't

sleep as well,
my dreams were more vivid,
I switched on the light,
and my sketches became great.

SIMON ARMITAGE

Zoom!

It begins as a house, an end terrace
in this case
   but it will not stop there. Soon it is
an avenue
   which cambers arrogantly past the Mechanics' Institute,
turns left
   at the main road without even looking
and quickly it is
   a town with all four major clearing banks,
a daily paper
   and a football team pushing for promotion.

On it goes, oblivious of the Planning Acts,
the green belts,
   and before we know it is out of our hands:
city, nation,
   hemisphere, universe, hammering out in all directions
until suddenly,
   mercifully, it is drawn aside through the eye
of a black hole
   and bulleted into a neighbouring galaxy, emerging
smaller and smoother
   than a billiard ball but weighing more than Saturn.

People stop me in the street, badger me
in the check-out queue
   and ask 'What is this, this that is so small
and so very smooth
   but whose mass is greater than the ringed planet?'
It's just words
   I assure them. But they will not have it.

The Space We Live In

The space we live in is too big for us to understand
any more than the hamper discerns its hasp,
and it's expanding at a rate now getting out of hand

even for those given to expand
on th'expanse. Cleopatra might have deduced from an asp
the space we live in is too big for us to understand

and clutched at the sand
as a cloak might clutch at its clasp.
That it's expanding at a rate now getting out of hand

may account for the looseness of the bellyband
on a chariot-horse that again and again strikes at the asp.
The space we live in is too big for us to understand

any more than the blacksmith can make sense of the brand
on his own forehead. Barely has a hoof met his rasp
than it's expanding at a rate now getting out of hand

like a chariot-team acting up the instant it's out-spanned.
When Cleopatra confides in the asp
the space we live in is too big for us to understand

it retorts with a poisonous gland
so she takes in only with her last gasp
that it's expanding at a rate now getting out of hand

and leaving her in some profound sense unmanned
by her complete failure to grasp
the space we live in is too big for us to understand
and it's expanding at a rate now getting out of hand.

NORMAN MacCAIG

Stars and Planets

Trees are cages for them: water holds its breath
To balance them without smudging on its delicate meniscus.
Children watch them playing in their heavenly playground;
Men use them to lug ships across oceans, through firths.

They seem so twinkle-still, but they never cease
Inventing new spaces and huge explosions
And migrating in mathematical tribes over
The steppes of space at their outrageous ease.

It's hard to think that the earth is one –
This poor sad bearer of wars and disasters
Rolls-Roycing round the sun with its load of gangsters,
Attended only by the loveless moon.

WILLIAM WORDSWORTH

from The Prelude

Conclusion: Book 13, ll. 10–65

It was a summer's night, a close warm night,
Wan, dull and glaring, with a dripping mist
Low-hung and thick that covered all the sky
Half threatening storm and rain; but on we went
Unchecked, being full of heart and having faith
In our tried pilot. Little could we see
Hemmed round on every side with fog and damp,
And, after ordinary travellers' chat
With our conductor, silently we sank
Each into commerce with his private thoughts.
Thus did we breast the ascent, and by myself
Was nothing either seen or heard the while
Which took me from my musings, save that once
The shepherd's cur did to his own great joy
Unearth a hedgehog in the mountain crags
Round which he made a barking turbulent.
This small adventure (for even such it seemed
In that wild place and at the dead of night)
Being over and forgotten, on we wound
In silence as before.

                   With forehead bent
Earthward, as if in opposition set
Against an enemy, I panted up
With eager pace, and no less eager thoughts.
Thus might we wear perhaps an hour away,
Ascending at loose distance each from each,
And I, as chanced, the foremost of the band –
When at my feet the ground appeared to brighten,

And with a step or two seemed brighter still;
Nor had I time to ask the cause of this,
For instantly a light upon the turf
Fell like a flash! I looked about, and lo,
The moon stood naked in the heavens at height
Immense above my head, and on the shore
I found myself of a huge sea of mist,
Which meek and silent rested at my feet.
A hundred hills their dusky backs upheaved
All over this still ocean; and beyond,
Far, far beyond, the vapours shot themselves
In headlands, tongues, and promontory shapes,
Into the sea – the real sea, that seemed
To dwindle and give up its majesty,
Usurped upon as far as sight could reach.
Meanwhile, the moon looked down upon this show
In single glory, and we stood, the mist
Touching our very feet. And from the shore
At distance not the third part of a mile
Was a blue chasm, a fracture in the vapour,
A deep and gloomy breathing-place through which
Mounted the roar of waters, torrents, streams
Innumerable, roaring with one voice!
The universal spectacle throughout
Was shaped for admiration and delight,
Grand in itself alone, but in that breach
Through which the homeless voice of waters rose,
That dark deep thoroughfare, had nature lodged
The soul, the imagination of the whole.

SEAMUS HEANEY

Westering
in California

I sit under Rand McNally's
'Official Map of the Moon' –
The colour of frogskin,
Its enlarged pores held

Open and one called
'Pitiscus' at eye level –
Recalling the last night
In Donegal, my shadow

Neat upon the whitewash
From her bony shine,
The cobbles of the yard
Lit pale as eggs.

Summer had been a free fall
Ending there,
The empty amphitheatre
Of the west. Good Friday

We had started out
Past shopblinds drawn on the afternoon,
Cars stilled outside still churches,
Bikes tilting to a wall;

We drove by,
A dwindling interruption
As clappers smacked
On a bare altar

And congregations bent
To the studded crucifix.
What nails dropped out that hour?
Roads unreeled, unreeled

Falling light as casts
Laid down
On shining waters.
Under the moon's stigmata

Six thousand miles away,
I imagine untroubled dust,
A loosening gravity,
Christ weighing by his hands.

SAMUEL TAYLOR COLERIDGE

from The Rime of the Ancient Mariner

The moving Moon went up the sky,
And nowhere did abide:
Softly she was going up,
And a star or two beside –

In his loneliness and fixedness he yearneth towards the journeying Moon, and the stars that still sojourn, yet still move onward; and every where the blue sky belongs to them, and is their appointed rest, and their native country and their own natural homes, which they enter unannounced, as lords that are certainly expected and yet there is a silent joy at their arrival.

Her beams bemocked the sultry main,
Like April hoar-frost spread;
But where the ship's huge shadow lay,
The charmèd water burnt alway
A still and awful red.

Beyond the shadow of the ship,
I watched the water-snakes:
They moved in tracks of shining white,
And when they reared, the elfish light
Fell off in hoary flakes.

By the light of the Moon he beholdeth God's creatures of the great calm.

Within the shadow of the ship,
I watched their rich attire:
Blue, glossy green, and velvet black,
They coiled and swam; and every track
Was a flash of golden fire.

O happy living things! no tongue
Their beauty might declare:
A spring of love gushed from my heart,
And I blessed them unaware:

Their beauty and their happiness.

He blesseth them in his heart.

Sure my kind saint took pity on me,
And I blessed them unaware.

The selfsame moment I could pray;
And from my neck so free
The Albatross fell off, and sank
Like lead into the sea.

The spell begins to break.

ALFRED LORD TENNYSON

from In Memoriam

And rise, O moon, from yonder down,
　　Till over down and over dale
　　All night the shining vapour sail
And pass the silent-lighted town,

The white-faced halls, the glancing rills,
　　And catch at every mountain head,
　　And o'er the friths that branch and spread
Their sleeping silver thro' the hills;

And touch with shade the bridal doors,
　　With tender gloom the roof, the wall;
　　And breaking let the splendour fall
To spangle all the happy shores

By which they rest, and ocean sounds,
　　And, star and system rolling past,
　　A soul shall draw from out the vast
And strike his being into bounds,

And, moved thro' life of lower phase,
　　Result in man, be born and think,
　　And act and love, a closer link
Betwixt us and the crowning race

Of those that, eye to eye, shall look
　　On knowledge; under whose command
　　Is Earth and Earth's, and in their hand
Is Nature like an open book;

No longer half-akin to brute,
       For all we thought and loved and did,
       And hoped, and suffer'd, is but seed
Of what in them is flower and fruit;

Whereof the man, that with me trod
       This planet, was a noble type
       Appearing ere the times were ripe,
That friend of mine who lives in God,

That God, which ever lives and loves,
       One God, one law, one element,
       And one far-off divine event,
To which the whole creation moves.

EMILY DICKINSON

'How Noteless Men, and Pleiads, Stand'

How noteless Men, and Pleiads, stand,
Until a sudden sky
Reveals the fact that One is rapt –
Forever from the Eye –

Members of the Invisible,
Existing, while we stare,
In Leagueless Opportunity,
O'ertakeless, as the Air –

Why didn't we detain Them?
The Heavens with a smile,
Sweep by our disappointed Heads
Without a syllable –

T.S. ELIOT

from Choruses from 'The Rock'

The Eagle soars in the summit of Heaven,
The Hunter with his dogs pursues his circuit.
O perpetual revolution of configured stars,
O perpetual recurrence of determined seasons,
O world of spring and autumn, birth and dying!
The endless cycle of idea and action,
Endless invention, endless experiment,
Brings knowledge of motion, but not of stillness;
Knowledge of speech, but not of silence;
Knowledge of words, and ignorance of the Word.
All our knowledge brings us nearer to our ignorance,
All our ignorance brings us nearer to death,
But nearness to death no nearer to God.
Where is the Life we have lost in living?
Where is the wisdom we have lost in knowledge?
Where is the knowledge we have lost in information?
The cycles of Heaven in twenty centuries
Bring us farther from God and nearer to the Dust.

HUGH MacDIARMID

The Bonnie Broukit Bairn

Mars is braw in crammasy,
Venus in a green silk goun,
The auld mune shak's her gowden feathers,
Their starry talk's a wheen o' blethers,
Nane for thee a thochtie sparin',
Earth, thou bonnie broukit bairn!
– *But greet, an' in your tears ye'll drown*
The haill clanjamfrie!

broukit, *neglected*; braw, *handsome*; crammasy, *crimson*; greet, *weep*

Lute Music

The earth will be going on a long time
Before it finally freezes;
Men will be on it; they will take names,
Give their deeds reasons.
We will be here only
As chemical constituents –
A small franchise indeed.
Right now we have lives,
Corpuscles, ambitions, caresses,
Like everybody had once –
All the bright neige d'antan people,
'Blithe Helen, white Iope, and the rest',
All the uneasy, remembered dead.

Here at the year's end, at the feast
Of birth, let us bring to each other
The gifts brought once west through deserts –
The precious metal of our mingled hair,
The frankincense of enraptured arms and legs,
The myrrh of desperate, invincible kisses –
Let us celebrate the daily
Recurrent nativity of love,
The endless epiphany of our fluent selves,
While the earth rolls away under us
Into unknown snows and summers,
Into untraveled spaces of the stars.

Notes on the Commissioned Poems

Julia Copus on 'Stars Moving Westwards in a Winter Garden', page 34
This poem arose directly out of my meeting with Malcolm Coe, Professor of Astronomy at Southampton University, who, by happy coincidence, teaches a course to the general public called 'Astronomy for Poets' in the very bookshop where we met for a coffee one cold November afternoon. In his words, the course 'is aimed at explaining the basic ideas about the universe to non-scientists without using the sophisticated language of professional science'. Malcolm's patient answers to my own questions about the way the seasons work sparked a memory of Anne Carson's observation that 'Perhaps the hardest thing about losing a lover is / to watch the year repeat its days'. After listening to Malcolm, it seemed to me that the movement of the universe and our place in it, the repetition of the days, the overlaying of memories, and our ultimate lack of control over the whole process, is every bit as consoling as it is distressing.

Greg Delanty on 'The Event Horizon', page 177
I was brought up Catholic in a Catholic world and as a child believed completely in heaven, purgatory, hell and limbo – though the mysterious declaration by the Vatican that limbo does not exist shook my faith as much as reading the existentialists in my late teens. Now I'm neither a believer nor a non-believer, not wanting to be categorised in any way, including agnostic. I tend toward non-belief, thinking of the afterlife of heaven, hell and purgatory as fantasy worlds. However, the work of astrophysicists like David Helfand on black holes, neutron stars and other phenomena opens up the possibility of such zones where time stops, etc. This is where 'The Event Horizon' comes from.

James Fenton on 'Cosmology: A Prologue', page 48
The poem emerged as a result of reading Pedro Ferreira's *The State of the Universe* at the same time as Barry Cunliffe's *Europe Between the*

Oceans, 9000 BC–AD 1000 – that is to say I was imagining the birth of cosmology in prehistory. Thinking in such huge periods, one imagines a question posed… and waiting thousands of years for an answer. At the same time, man is on the move, looking for new places to support him, and requiring the night sky for navigation.

Leontia Flynn on 'The Full Moon and the Ferris Wheel', page 67
I had looked up some information on the moon, and the facts that stuck were that the moon and the earth rotated in unison, so that we pretty much never see the far side, and that this was the result of a force that locked them together. I had a vision of the planet and moon turning like a kind of fan belt – which is perhaps at odds with the traditional view of the moon as mysterious and feminine. Likewise the moon as the object at the heart of the Russian/US space race seems macho and unromantic rather than elemental. When I contacted Mark Bailey of the Armagh Planetarium, he mentioned some of the shapes we discern in the moon: the rabbit, the kicking donkey, and (apparently) J. F. Kennedy. The Ferris Wheel is one recently erected in Belfast: there was a giant harvest moon the weekend it first appeared.

John Kinsella on 'The Light Echo of Supernova 1987A', page 129
[From email exchange between John Kinsella and David Malin.]
JK: working with refrains for the echoes at the moment.
p.s. i love the lichen-like textures within the photo 'surface' – the echoes of life therein coupled with the immensity of the shockwaves. a paradox. i like the paradox, ambiguity, tautology, contradiction etc… the impact of beauty. i also see the dilations of the eye. which must reach a point of total expansion before it turns back (cancelling out, altering etc)? sorry, making poems here…

DM: Well let me give you some more echoes.
The gritty, textured appearance of the photograph is the result of trying to subtract one image from another. The lichen-like structures are photographic noise, echoes of the silver grains that captured the ancient light. Lichen itself is both an echo and noise. It's an echo of

some of the earliest, most primitive green plants and it is ubiquitous, appearing almost everywhere there is sunlight and water, a kind of subliminal background.

The supernova that made the flash of light created vast amounts of elements heavier than iron, which cannot be made in better-behaved stars like the Sun, so the iron, tin, gold and platinum and the silver that made the picture possible are a tangible echo of supernovae that exploded before the Sun and planets formed, 4.5 billion years ago. More remarkable is the idea that you are looking down a time tube to the light echo, an ellipse with you and me at one end of it and the supernova, 170,000 light years distant, at the other. The light echoes are lightplay on the walls of this tube, where it meets dust in space. All this is an effect of the finite travel time of light, and none of it is visible to the eye.

JK: I've written about the life echoes of lichen re the image/s. actually, written a lot about lichen over the years. love the stuff. the encodings of life, eh!

Antjie Krog on 'I Am, Because You Are', page 109

I wrote the poem during my nine-month stay at the Wissenschaftskolleg zu Berlin – far away from the abundance of the southern skies of South Africa. I was contacted by Hans Zinnecker who was fully taken up in several field trips to the North and South Americas. He sent me a postcard of the birth of a twin star which he had discovered, symmetrically pushed out by an unobservable protostar near the Horsehead Nebula in the Orion constellation. It was called: HH212.

I was in deep trouble. As I read about his discovery, I realised that I had no Afrikaans vocabulary to express this. Being away from home meant that I could not look for Afrikaans astronomers or books nearby. I followed two strategies. on the Internet I came across an Afrikaans website on stars, but it did not carry the latest developments that would include Zinneker's discovery. I asked my translator in Utrecht and publisher in Amsterdam to send me Dutch books and astronomy magazines. From these sources I could forge a rather extensive Afrikaans astronomy vocabulary while enriching my life enormously by reading extensively about the miracle of the universe. This, of course, had to gestate and be absorbed into the creative bloodstream before it could become internal inspiration.

When the poem was written, I translated it into English and this version was sent to Hans. Between one trip and another he had two days in Berlin and we had coffee in Kurfürstendammstrasse. He had many questions about the meaning of the poem and then discussed in detail the essence of his discovery: symmetry. As I was rewriting specifically that part of the poem, it turned by itself into a visual symmetrical form with which Hans was very pleased.

Nick Laird on 'The Effects', page 165

I corresponded with Paul Murdin, the treasurer of the Royal Astronomical Society, and he was kind enough to receive me at the Society's offices in Burlington House in Piccadilly. Paul has written many great books on the cosmos (including *Catalogue of the Universe*, a title I used in the poem), and in 1971 he discovered a black hole in Cygnus X-1. Our discussions in person and on email ranged widely but I was always drawn back to the idea of what we could and couldn't see, of what lay within our light spectrum and what lay outside it. I asked Paul at one point how you could observe a black hole and he said you couldn't, not directly, though often a black hole appeared in tandem with another star, and you could tell the black hole was there because of a disturbance in space-time. You could see the black hole pulling gas down on itself. He described it as a small dog running through a crowd, where you can't see the animal, only the movement of the people. I tried to couple that idea with a few others and the poem 'The Effects' is the result. I should also say that the first part draws heavily on a paragraph of Wallace Stevens.

Bill Manhire on 'Herschel at the Cape', page 44

I was partnered with the astronomer and science writer Marilyn Head. When we first met, we talked mainly about Southern Hemisphere astronomy. At some point the talk came around to Sir John Herschel. I had heard of William Herschel, and of his sister Caroline, but not of

John. As Marilyn talked about John, it slowly dawned on me that she was in love with him – true! – and as I began to read more about him, it became clear why he is held in such great and universal affection. Marilyn found me a copy of the journal he kept during the 1830s when he spent several years at the Cape of Good Hope completing his father's catalogue of stars (*Herschel at the Cape: Diaries and Correspondence of Sir John Herschel, 1834–1838*, ed. David S. Evans et al, Austin and London, University of Texas Press, 1969). I felt lifted by the rich variety of his interests, and by the sheer joy which accompanies his steady observations of the stars. He is a wonderful instance of human happiness.

Kathryn Maris on 'Why', page 200

I like to write about Big Things, the biggest in fact: God Himself. But I'm not a believer in the usual sense. *My* God is my own hubristic invention. He is what I tell Him to be: a pile of leaves, a psychoanalyst, or a man who gives you a dodgy package.

What does this have to do with astrophysics? When your mind is on God, it tends to be on science, too, whether you disapprove of it or respect it. Like most poets, I admire scientists. But when asked what kind of physicist I wanted to work with, I didn't know. I looked outside, saw a cloud of gnats in the garden, and suggested 'particles'. And that's how I was paired with Frank Close, the Oxford-based particle physicist and writer.

I liked Frank from the moment I entered his name on Amazon. His nine or so books seemed a smörgåsbord of existential angst, with titles like *End: Cosmic Catastrophe and the Fate of the Universe* and *The Void*. The one I chose first was *Lucifer's Legacy: The Meaning of Asymmetry*, which argues that despite the attractiveness and apparent abundance of symmetry in our world, the unsung hero of our existence is asymmetry. Frank writes, 'If the Creation had been perfect, and its symmetry had remained unblemished, nothing that we now know would ever have been.'

He offers examples of asymmetry in the natural world, like a man's testicles (the left hangs lower than the right), building up to a mind-bending discussion of the Higgs boson, popularly called the 'God particle'. He explains that this 'God particle', if it exists, ruined the balance between matter and antimatter in favour of matter. Without the Higgs boson, or something similar, matter would have been annihilated by antimatter and the universe wouldn't have stood a chance.

I'm oversimplifying of course, and I simplified the theory further by writing a poem in the voice of God. Instead of 'Let there be light', he commands 'Let there be imperfection'. The poem is in syllabics; that is, in lines containing a prescribed number of syllables. Each of my lines has three syllables (which I chose for the Biblical connotations) except for the line 'imperfection', which has four.

Eventually I rejected the poem, sensing that Frank was unimpressed too, though he was too polite to say so. So I turned to his other books, one of which asks: 'What was God doing the night before Creation?'

While my brain was agitating over this, Frank and I set up our meeting. During our three-hour chat at Paddington Station, he showed me the draft of an essay he was writing for the *London Review of Books* about time travel. In it, he mentions the paradoxical idea that the universe may have formed itself out of the future.

I sometimes jog in the Paddington Recreation Ground, where there's a bandstand that looks like a pagoda. One day, a man in a wheelchair was sitting in the bandstand, and I found myself projecting on him my assumptions about disability. He was talking to someone I couldn't see, repeatedly using a word that sounded like 'Why', as though he were railing against God. But when I went closer, I realised he was speaking Arabic.

My skewed interpretation of the man in the bandstand connected somehow with Frank's ideas and questions – 'What was God doing the night before Creation?' and 'Did the universe form itself out of the future?' – and became my poem for this anthology.

The commission turned two-way when Frank emailed to ask if I could suggest a metaphor for the book he was working on, *Antimatter*. He wanted to know how I, a layperson, view the relationship between matter and antimatter. I had a series of fatuous ideas like 'good and evil', 'God and Satan', 'dark and light', until I thought of Cain and Abel. I wrote back and said, 'Cain and Abel are siblings, and their parents are the Original Parents (i.e. the Big Bang) and one sibling kills off the other.'

Maybe my idea will turn up in *Antimatter*, but I doubt it.

After this exchange, I walked to my bookshelf in the direction of *Beowulf* like a robot with a homing device. I took the book down and re-read it with a vague idea of Grendel as antimatter, and was startled to discover that Grendel was a descendant of Cain. My point is that my collaboration with Frank is the commission that keeps on commissioning. He has sent me to a strange, faraway place, and I have decided to stay for a while.

John McAuliffe on 'Arguing about Stars near Inch', page 31

In May I spent an illuminating afternoon with Prof. John Dyson in Manchester, *illuminating* because of the 'pretty pictures' of stars he brought with him on his laptop, but also because of the way he walked me through the difficulties of his research in star formation, patiently explaining the terminology and descriptive terms he used. John's explanations did not focus on astronomy's achievements; instead, he repeatedly returned to the puzzle and mysteries of star formation, and how astronomers have diversely approached this problem and all of its variables. He also described paradigm shifts which have transformed astronomy in the past century, including the story of how magnetic fields had emerged, disappeared and re-emerged as a serious area of study.

Just as fascinating were his asides about his happy involvement with Armagh's cleric-dominated Observatory, his curiosity about how a poem might emerge from this material, and his impatience with some of the 'cuter' names used by recent astronomers for their discoveries. When I went to the Aran Islands and then Kerry soon after our meeting, and wrote this poem, I found it hard to resist the seductive new vocabulary to which I'd been introduced. But, mulling over the re-emergence of 'magnetic fields', or new ways of thinking about the role of 'dust' in John's research area, made me look again at what was in front of me, the beaches and trees of the western coast, and think a lot more clearly about how slippery, *un*definitive and *mortal* the theories could be...

Jamie McKendrick on 'Out There', page 163

A few weeks before meeting Dr Kevin Fong, I'd happened to watch on TV *In the Shadow of the Moon*, a film directed by David Sington which tells the story of the moon voyages, and had been struck by how that experience had remained undimmed and transformative for the US astronauts.

During our meeting in an outdoor café in central London, through the noise of terrestrial traffic – especially that of an old Czech motorbike that seemed to be orbiting the block – Dr Fong spoke with eloquent detail about a whole range of phenomena connected with space travel, from the effects of microgravity on hand-to-eye co-ordination to its impact on bone density and muscle: how the body gradually wastes in space. I was also intrigued by his account of the differing ethos of the Russian and US space programmes and of the various arguments as to where outer space actually begins. We discussed the film and the testimonies of the various astronauts, one of whom had sounded uncannily close to that moment in *Paradiso* where Dante looks back down to the Earth from the Heaven of Saturn and sees 'L'aiuola che ci fa tanto feroci…' (The little patch which makes us all so fierce).

I had covered a large manila envelope in micro-script trying to keep up with Dr Fong's energetic speech, and was expecting far more of a tussle with all of this almost too vivid material – to be honest, I hardly expected to be able to write the poem at all. Without needing to look at the notes, though, I began writing the next day and the poem quickly found its own shape. After that, the only significant change was suggested by Dr Fong, who noticed an incorrect detail: I had misheard 'step' for 'sleep', most likely the fault of the motorcyclist. Dr Fong's stories and explanations have made their way into the poem, together with a trace of the film and that line from Dante.

Robert Pinsky on 'The Procession', page 81

The astronomer James Moran and his colleagues were adept at giving a rather ignorant outsider some sense of their intellectually exciting work with the Submillimeter Array of antennae. During that lucid explanation I also learned a striking, though incidental, fact about the Array: its components, eight large but mobile instruments atop the mountain Mauna Kea, wheel about to change their configuration, there in Hawaii, driven by the hand of someone at a computer in Massachusetts.

To a tourist of knowledge like me, those two degrees of distance – intergalactic and intercontinental, both mediated by invisible means of communication – suggested two orders of reality, one on warm earth and one in cold space. Massachusetts is remote from Hawaii, and both are remote from Aldebaran. But to say so teases or stretches the very concept of 'remote'.

Like the celebrated short film made by Ray and Charles Eames, *Powers of Ten*, the Submillimeter Array discloses an intricate, enabling dance between the all-but-unthinkably large and the all-but-unthinkably small. That dance includes the processors and memory chips within the digital computer; it includes the motorised antennae with their twenty-foot reflectors as they waltz about funnelling information into central receptors a micron or two wide. Also part of the dance is the hulking, forty-year-old industrial machine tool that mills the precise, infinitesimal channels within those receptors. Above all, the dance includes invisible little waves that travel across the universe and across time. The kinds of mediation and remoteness, the orders of survival across distance, seemed as multiple, indeed infinite, as Hindu cosmology.

I was reminded of a cartoon I like: the full-page rectangle is filled mostly by a vast night sky studded with innumerable stars. Gazing up at that hyperbolic, heavenly display from one corner of the rectangle are two people. The caption: 'It makes me realize how insignificant you are.'

This brilliant joke exposes a cliché by ambush and reversal. One aim of poetry is to touch the generative reality underlying truism or cliché: possibly to find, in apparent disproportions of scale, in the interpenetration of psyche and cosmos, some heartfelt apprehension of insignificance and significance.

Deryn Rees-Jones on 'A Dream of Constellations', pages 181, 230

I became interested in the idea that over millions of years the constellations must, with the birth and death of new stars, have shifted their patterns. The narratives of the sky – the resonant myths attached to the things we see there – seemed a long way away from the rather depersonalised and ever-changing, endlessly expanding universe. The night sky is such a source of constancy, if only to the naked eye, that I imagined the crisis in an individual life might get projected, as time sped up, onto the sky. This would mean the breaking up or destroying of those famous patterns and stories. I also knew from first-hand experience – the recent death of my father, the serious illness of my husband – that the stories we tell ourselves about our own lives are fragile and open to radical retelling in the blink of an eye. Thinking about the constellations returned me to Mallarmé's poem *Un coup de dés* (1897), a poem which experiments with textual layout, mimicking the patterns of the stars. When I talked to Professor Morison he spoke about how important radiowaves were in modern astronomy. He also mentioned how some astronomers had been involved in sending out Morse code messages to space – to whoever was there to receive them. My father had been a keen amateur radio operator, and I remembered as a child sitting at the kitchen table as he practised his Morse code. My own navigation of this period of crisis seemed too immediately personal to be put simply into words, and so I transposed the whole poem into Morse code. The fact that written-down Morse, at least to my poet's eye, looked in itself like a depiction of a night sky busy with stars, added to my sense of making the poem something other than itself.

Neil Rollinson on 'The Very Small Baseline Group Convenes at the Cat and Fiddle', page 98

Anita Richards is a radio astronomer who works at Jodrell Bank, Britain's biggest radio telescope. I met Anita over coffee in her common room at Manchester University, where she took me through a few of the latest ideas in radio astronomy, and some of the basics too, which were hard enough to get my head around: frequency, wavelength, red-shifts and baselines. It was going to be difficult. I hadn't a clue how I was going to approach this poem. However, I was in the pub with an old friend and he told me about how, as a child, he was taken to a pub garden somewhere on the edge of the moors from where he could see Jodrell Bank in the gloaming, as the sun went down, and the image had stuck in his imagination ever since. He thought the pub was called 'The Neptune' or something fanciful like that, though I couldn't find a pub called that anywhere near. However, this was all I needed to get me started: pub – garden – beer – the mystical, alchemical process of the brew – drunkenness – the ur-world of imagination. Anita had told me about the Array telescopes they were using and developing now, where you use a load of antennas or small dishes spread over a distance and then amalgamate the information, extrapolate the input, and in effect create a huge telescope out of many small ones. I just saw the empty beer glasses on the table as being part of such a telescope and off I went. I was minded of the poetry of Peter Redgrove and how he might approach a poem like this in a similar way: magic, potency and the all-embracing nature of material. When I put this to Anita, I thought she'd think 'What the hell is this guy on?', but she was very enthusiastic and seemed to think the idea was very fitting, as she said, 'there is a history of radio interferometry at Jodrell Bank being carried out at pubs', and she sent me a paper about the so-called Very Long Baseline Group, who developed such a telescope in the 60s by placing a receiver in the garden of a pub on the edge of the moors overlooking Jodrell Bank. Bingo! Eureka! Don't you just love that kind of serendipity – this is always part of the creative process, and always will be.

The pub was actually called 'The Cat and Feather', and not 'The Neptune', but I'd found my poem. The process seemed akin to what happens in radio astronomy; you sweep the skies looking for something that makes sense of the universe and eventually you find it, or you find parts of it, or you find more questions, which seems to be what happens when you write poems, and that's why I believe there's a connection between poetry and science. We're in the same business. We're just trying to find out what we are and what makes us tick. What the hell the world and the universe is all about.

Tom Sleigh on 'For a Spacesuit Set Adrift', page 154

When Auden talks about paradise being a place that includes obsolete mining equipment, like an overshot waterwheel, my paradise would be one full of space junk: decommissioned satellites, rocket boosters, gantries that fall away as lift-off occurs. Even the space age moves toward inconsequence. And so my poem is a kind of elegy based on an online image of a spacesuit cast adrift from the International Space Station in a ham radio experiment. The suit was stuffed full of old clothes and shoved out the airlock.

I was aided in writing it by Neil Tyson's book *Death by Black Hole*. I adapted a phrase from one of Tyson's essays about radio transmission, as well as a passage about the violence and chaos of space. And the general sense of loneliness and literal emptiness of space that Tyson talks about dovetailed with what I felt when I saw the empty spacesuit in the NASA image.

Cut off from the mother ship, the spacesuit has some of the glamour and loneliness of a tintype – as if it were a pioneer bride drifting across the photographer's blank screen as through a void. Barely separated from the hands that gave her away, already she is subject to earth's gravity and the friction of the atmosphere that will burn her to nothing.

On one level, then, the poem is an elegy – for my mother-in-law, who recently died, though the poem never reaches for a one-to-one correspondence. And on another level, the suit's strangely homemade, homely, almost maternal presence seems to domesticate the void surrounding it, and to lend perspective to the monstrous, blue-black curve of earth's ocean rising up.

'A Dream of Constellations' by Deryn Rees-Jones, see pages 181 and 227

When the months that were left could be held in our hands
I wanted to speak, but I could not. The astrocytal cells
that formed and grew inside your brain
following heart lines, speech lines, bedding in,
bringing you visions, disrupting your speech,
brought us a night that was suddenly known,
but not as itself. And so, like a dream about to be spoken,
silence buried itself in me. In this new pitch,
the navigated darkness of our life,
this telling and untelling of the world,
Time sped and slowed. The constellations shifted
bringing us messages in particles of dust and light.
Together we looked up to the sky
as Ursa Minor became the headless bear,
the twin sons of Castor and Pollux, unexcellent, unsweet,
buried themselves beneath the earth,
and Vela's sail unfurled, became ragged.
Sagittarius the archer staggered wounded
ripped his arm on a jagged star, unnamed for this instant;
together we wept for Berenice
with her one breast, with her shorn-off hair.
And as Time was slinking, doing its business,
the fiery empyreal nature of things
became the thing on which we most depended.
It was a new world, our night sky,
and I'd like to think the story of what lived between us then
expanded in the moment of our looking:
charting new maps in the darkness, allowing us to trust
that we might live by the light of the stars and their
reseedings, those wild celestial fields, which
as we looked up and back across time
hovered in the dots and dashes
between what is and was.

Acknowledgements

The editors and the Calouste Gulbenkian Foundation would like to thank the following poets and publishers for permission to reproduce their work. While every effort has been made to secure permission to reprint material protected by copyright, they will be pleased to make good any omissions brought to their attention in future printings of this book.

Diane Ackerman, 'We Are Listening' from *Jaguar of Sweet Laughter: New and selected poems* (Random House 1991); Fleur Adcock, 'The Ex-Queen Among the Astronomers' from *Poems 1960–2000* (Bloodaxe Books 2000); Simon Armitage, 'Zoom!' from *ZOOM!* (Bloodaxe Books 1989); W.H. Auden, 'After Reading a Child's Guide to Modern Physics' and 'Moon Landing' from *Collected Poems* (Faber and Faber Ltd 2004); Leo Aylen, 'Orbiting Pluto' from *Dancing the Impossible: New and Selected Poems* (University of Salzburg Press 1997) copyright © Leo Aylen; George Bradley, 'About Planck Time' from *Terms To Be Met* (Yale University Press 1986); Billy Collins, 'Earthling' from *The Apple That Astonished Paris* (University of Arkansas Press 1988, 1996), copyright © by Billy Collins, used by permission of the University of Arkansas Press, www.uapress.com; Greg Delanty, 'The Alien' from *Collected Poems 1986–2006* (Carcanet Press Ltd 2006); Patric Dickinson, 'Jodrell Bank' from *The World I See* (Chatto & Windus 1960), reprinted by permission of David Dickinson and Virginia Lindley; Alan Dugan, 'Prothalamion of Quantum Mechanics and Astrophysics' from *Poems Seven: New and complete poetry* (Seven Story Press 2001); T.S. Eliot, 'Choruses from "The Rock"' from *Collected Poems 1909–1962* (Faber and Faber Ltd 2002); Alison Hawthorne Deming, 'Mt Lemmon, Steward Observatory 1990' from *Science and Other Poems* (Louisiana State University Press 1994), copyright © by Alison Hawthorne Deming, reprinted by permission of Louisiana State University Press; Rebecca Elson, 'Let There Always Be Light' from *A Responsibility to Awe* (Carcanet Press Ltd 2001); William Empson, 'Letter I' from *The Complete Poems* (Penguin 2000),

Cosmos Ballroom (1)' from *Blues* (Jonathan Cape 2004), reprinted by permission of The Random House Group Ltd; W.B. Yeats, 'The Song of the Happy Shepherd' from *The Collected Poems of W.B. Yeats* (Prentice Hall & IBD 1996), reprinted by permission of A P Watt Ltd on behalf of Gráinne Yeats.

Index of Poets

Maurice Riordan

Maurice Riordan received the 2007 Michael Hartnett Award for his latest collection, *The Holy Land* (Faber), while previous collections, *A Word from the Loki* and *Floods*, were nominated for a T. S. Eliot Prize and a Whitbread Book Award. His other publications include *A Quark for Mister Mark: 101 Poems About Science*, the ecological anthology *Wild Reckoning*, and *Hart Crane*, which has recently appeared in Faber's 'Poet to Poet' series. Born in Lisgoold, Co. Cork, he lives in London and edits *Poetry London*.

Jocelyn Bell Burnell

Jocelyn Bell Burnell DBE is Visiting Professor of Astrophysics at the University of Oxford. As a post-graduate student at Cambridge, she was involved in the discovery of pulsars, for which her supervisor won a Nobel Prize. She has received numerous awards for her work, in the UK and USA, and is President of the Institute of Physics. She has long collected poems on astronomy and contributed to the OUP anthology *Contemporary Poetry and Contemporary Science* in 2006.

Also published by the Calouste Gulbenkian Foundation

Wild Reckoning: An anthology provoked by Rachel Carson's *Silent Spring*

Edited by John Burnside and Maurice Riordan

Wild Reckoning is an anthology inspired by the fortieth anniversary of Rachel Carson's controversial and prophetic book *Silent Spring*, which warned against the indiscriminate use of pesticides and its consequences for the environment. The anthology features poems commissioned from leading poets – including Simon Armitage, Paul Farley, Linda Gregerson and Deryn Rees-Jones – which were the fruit of discussions with scientists such as Richard Fortey and John Sulston. It also brings to the fore poems, both contemporary and from the past, which, while belonging to the great tradition of English nature poetry, express a concern for the fragility of living things.

A Poetry Book Society Special Commendation, *Wild Reckoning* was chosen by the Government's former Chief Scientific Adviser, Sir David King, to take to his imaginary Desert Island.

£7.50 pbk ISBN 978 1 903080 00 9 (2004)

Signs and Humours: The Poetry of Medicine

Edited by Lavinia Greenlaw

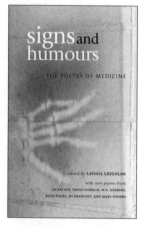

Signs and Humours brings together 100 poems written over the last 2,000 years to show how one of the most basic human concerns – the body – has continued to fascinate and agitate poets. Their pre-occupations are brought right up to date in 22 specially commissioned poems, the result of discussions with leading doctors and scientists about contemporary bio-medical practice, which include deliberations on the pathologies of our time, from autism and infertility to pancreatitis and Post-Traumatic Stress Disorder. Whether it's Horace complaining about garlic playing havoc with his digestive system, Grey Gowrie recovering from a heart transplant or Jo Shapcott demonstrating – a lack of – latent inhibition, this anthology explores the questions that arise when we are forced to stop and consider our physical selves.

£8.50 pbk ISBN 978 1 903080 09 2 (2007)

Both titles are available from Central Books, 99 Wallis Road, London E9 5LN
tel: 0845 458 9911, fax: 0845 458 9912
website: www.centralbooks.co.uk